AF712251

REAL-WORLD ECONOMICS

COMPLEX AND MESSY

by Mark Akers

UNIVERSITY OF INDIANAPOLIS PRESS

Copyright © 2014 by the University of Indianapolis Press
All rights reserved. No portion of this book may be produced in any form or by any means without written permission of the University of Indianapolis Press.

Planning: Phylis Lan Lin, University of Indianapolis Press Executive Director
Layout: Edgar Huang
Cover design: Faith Charli Dee and Edgar Huang
University of Indianapolis Press Logo: Detail from a painting by Au Ho-nien
Press Editors: Phylis Lan Lin, Peter Noot & Stephanie Seifert Stringham
Press Reviewers: Phylis Lan Lin, Douglas R. Woodwell & Milind Thakar
Indexer: Marilyn Augst, Prairie Moon Indexing
Press Assistant to the Executive Director: Elaine Bradburn

Printed in the United States

18 17 16 15 14 5 4 3 2 1

ISBN: 978-1-880938-83-6

Published by
University of Indianapolis Press
University of Indianapolis
1400 East Hanna Avenue
Indianapolis, IN 46227-3697
Fax: (317) 788-3480
Phone: (317) 788-3288
E-mail: lin@uindy.edu
http://www.uindy.edu/universitypress

This is for my students.

Mark Akers has taken the discussion of economies in one of the newer directions being discussed. There are many economists writing useful and meaningful books about these topics, but to examine them in the light of complexity and the resilience of economies is needed. One reviewer called the book "engaging." I agree. It is a timely and well-written view of how economies work.

—John Mutz, Former Lt. Governor, State of Indiana

Mark Akers has written an excellent explanation of how economies really work. Standard economic theory will continue to serve us well, but understanding why the economy changes so quickly and how it adapts to unexpected shocks is very important for business and employment. Akers writes clearly and his examples make a complex subject understandable.

—Bill Warren, CEO, Direct Employers Association, Former President of Monster.com

Many economists look at the economy from the outside in or even from the top down, but Mark Akers' experience as an economic development professional gives him unique experience, allowing him to see the economy from the inside out and to share a perspective that is both practical and applicable.

—Lee Lewellen, CEO, Indiana Economic Development Association

TABLE OF CONTENTS

Acknowledgments xiii

Synopsis xv

Introduction 1

1. Briefly, the Long-Term Sand Pile 3

2. GDP 13

3. Why Are Some Countries So Poor and Others So Rich? 23

4. It Gets Complex 31

5. Keynes and Messy Business Cycles 55

6. The Maximum Sustainable Economy 71

7. What to Do 87

8. As We All Know, Change Is Bad 99

References 103

About the Author 105

About the University of Indianapolis Press 108

Books from the University of Indianapolis Press (1992–2003) 109

University of Indianapolis Press Book List (2004–2014) 110

Index 111

Too large a portion of "mathematical" economics are mere concoctions, as imprecise as the initial assumptions they rest on, which allow the author to lose sight of the complexities and interdependencies of the real world in a maze of pretentious and unhelpful symbols.

—John Maynard Keynes

Bak liked to pass along a quote from the nineteenth-century novelist Victor Hugo as a prescient summary of the idea: "How do we know that the creations of the worlds are not determined by falling grains of sand." What if the real world was like this, precariously balanced between stability and chaos? Bak wondered. If the logic of such a complex system could be penetrated, even a little bit, there might be no limit to what you could create. The world wasn't just a slew of senseless randomness; it just required a new and different way of calculating.

—Joshua Cooper Ramo, *The Age of the Unthinkable*

ACKNOWLEDGMENTS

In Malcolm Gladwell's book *Outliers: The Story of Success*, he writes that it takes about 10,000 hours of practice to gain a level of mastery of anything. Thus, if you put in about 20 hours a week practicing and learning your craft before you actually perform, mastery takes about 10 years. If that is true, then I owe a great deal to many people who have taught and helped me for the 10 years or more that I have been studying and teaching economics and public policy, aside from the 20 years of learning how economies actually work through my time working with cities in several states, especially Indiana, to help them organize, build, and create environments that created jobs and investment. Those who set me on this path include Dr. George Bullion, now Emeritus, at Purdue University, Fort Wayne, who was my tough master's thesis advisor and friend, who showed me that I could, in fact, follow ideas and see where they lead, and Richard T. Doermer, retired Chairman of the Board of Indiana Bank and Trust, who sent me from the bank to help start Fort Wayne's first economic development program. I have to include John Mutz, the former lieutenant governor of Indiana, a Republican who hired me away from the Democratic mayor of Fort Wayne to run the economic development programs for the State of Indiana, and who showed me what a true public servant was like. Then there is Jane Lambert, who first hired me to teach at Indiana University, Indianapolis, and put me to work teaching commercial law, which soon morphed into teaching many courses in the Kelley School of Business as well as in the School of Public and Environmental Affairs. I would add Dr. Matt Will, Associate Professor at the University of Indianapolis in the School of Business, whose first words to me included "Would you like to go to China?" and Dr. Sheela Yadav, former Dean of the School of Business at UIndy, who became a great friend and encourager and who expanded my teaching roles at UIndy and in China. And high among this group is Dr. Phylis Lan Lin at UIndy, who heads the International Partnerships and Asian Programs at UIndy and who has been my teacher and biggest supporter in making my China experiences so meaningful. Phylis is also Executive Director of the University of Indianapolis Press and has been very generous with her help and encouragement.

Without my wife, Cindy, I would not be doing any of this. For more than 44 years, her love, encouragement, and sacrifices for our family and my career have been far too numerous and too great to mention in this small space.

SYNOPSIS

This book examines economies as complex adaptive systems. Economies are made of innumerable parts that have different functions and require us to make choices among many alternatives. Economies include ordinary and exceptional people who live in all kinds of circumstances, all with their own resources, cultures, and set of rules they either must follow or choose to follow. Economies also include the institutions that people form, such as nations, governments, companies, corporations, schools, charities, social clubs, and many more. Economics is thus a way of describing how all of these parts work together and separately in order to get and spend money. In other words, economics is a behavioral science that focuses on what we do with money and why we do it.

With all these moving and thinking parts, trying to describe this system with any level of accuracy is difficult. To predict what these parts will do next is nearly impossible; however, if we can see why prediction is nearly impossible, we can better understand the descriptions and predictions we try to make.

A fairly precise definition of complex systems can be, well, complex. Melanie Mitchel describes complexity as groups of single entities, on their own, organizing themselves in ways that create patterns of behavior, and that sometimes evolve and learn. Thus, complex systems may start with no organized system or patterns but soon develop both, with no central command telling them what to do or how to do it. Because some complex systems evolve and learn, they can change their environments. In our case, we are most interested in what our complex system does with money.

Our global economy is a complex system creating apparently random patterns of behavior, but patterns that are based on different histories, cultures, technologies, and political decisions. These different patterns of behavior end up affecting people in other parts of the world because of how connected we now are through global markets, manufacturing and logistics systems, and the movement of money and people. When one economy has problems, so too can others. When economies try to adapt, they also learn and evolve into something new that will suit the changing economic environment. In other words, the global economy is acting like a complex adaptive system, and predicting what it is doing or will do is equally complex and challenging.

Additionally, the individual parts of complex system at some point will start to fall into synchronized patterns so that their actions are happening in concert with the actions of others. When we see this happen in an economy, the results are seen in the business cycles that often drive the expansions and contractions of economies over time.

If business and government must plan for, operate in, and try to affect this complex environment, what should they do? The answers are as wide-ranging as the complexity of the environment, but the basic answer is to make the economy even more complex. Why? For two primary reasons. First, the driving force of economic growth is innovation, and innovation thrives in a diverse environment where people and ideas from many places are brought together in some way, physically or through technology. There is much evidence that surprisingly new ways of doing things, of thinking, of inventing, and most other human activity occur when people from a variety of circumstances and experiences share in an open environment. More economic complexity is a key feature of this phenomenon.

Second, complex systems will adapt in the face of shocks, whether positive or negative. The system is already more complex than we expect, and the good or bad events in one part of the world will spread to other parts of the world (contagion). Thus, most economies—national, regional, and local—will have to develop their abilities to bounce back from the negative shocks (resilience). Resilience is a short-term reaction to a negative shock. It results from what is already in place in the economy—the characteristics of the workforce, the kinds of businesses, the amount of foreign trade the businesses do, wage rates, how much of the economy is based on durable-goods manufacturing, the culture, and more. Thus, governments that react to shocks by putting in place new tax incentives and infrastructure improvements will be disappointed. Resilience can be enhanced only when the needed changes are in place because of ongoing long-term planning in a rapidly changing environment.

This approach of examining economies as complex adaptive systems covers a lot of territory. This book covers a number of those topics, some in more depth than others. It is not meant to give a complete picture of the global economy but introduces several concepts that will hopefully give the reader a feel for the complexity of economies in the world today.

INTRODUCTION

This book examines economies as complex systems. Economies are made of innumerable parts that have different functions and involve choices among many alternatives. Economies include ordinary and exceptional people who live in all kinds of circumstances, each with his or her own resources, cultures, and set of rules that he or she either *must* follow or *choose* to follow. Economies also includes the institutions that people form, such as nations, governments, companies, corporations, schools, charities, and social clubs. Thus, economics is a way of describing how all of these parts work together and separately to get and spend money. In other words, economics is a behavioral science that focuses on what we do with money and why.

With all these moving and thinking parts, trying to describe this system with any level of accuracy is difficult. To predict what these parts will do next is nearly impossible; however, if we can see why prediction is nearly impossible, we can better understand the descriptions and predictions we try to make.

You may not be surprised to learn that a fairly precise definition of complex systems can be, well, complex. As we will discuss in more detail later, Melanie Mitchell describes complexity as groups of single entities, on their own, organizing themselves in ways that create patterns of behavior, and that sometimes evolve and learn. Thus, complex systems may start with no organized systems or patterns but soon develop both, with no central command telling them what to do or how to do it. Because some complex systems evolve and learn, they can change their environments. In our case, we are most interested in what our complex system does with money.

The idea for this book developed slowly over several months. As a professor at the University of Indianapolis (UIndy), I teach primarily economics and international business. UIndy also sends me to China to teach. In addition, I also teach public policy and law courses at Indiana University in the School of Public and Environmental Affairs as an adjunct professor. Prior to teaching, I had been in government for several years, managing Indiana's economic programs meant to help cities and towns attract and develop companies and economic activity, as well as managing the state's offices in Europe and

Asia. I had seen firsthand how complex economic systems are, especially as companies and governments try to relate each other's economies and systems.

Although the textbooks and other materials I used in my classes and as references for research and writing were very good for their purposes, I found relatively few that provided an overall description of how complex the economic systems were, why they were that way, and how complexity goes a long way in explaining why economic forecasts are very often wrong. We also need to define what a complex system is and how it fits into economics. Filling that void became the purpose of this book.

Our global economy is a complex system creating apparently random patterns of behavior, but patterns that are based on different histories, cultures, technologies, and political decisions. These different patterns of behavior end up affecting people in other parts of the world because of how connected we now are through global markets, manufacturing and logistics systems, and the movement of money and people. When one economy has problems, so do most others. When economies try to adapt, they also learn and evolve into something new that will suit the changing economic environment. In other words, the global economy is acting like a complex system, and predicting what it is doing or will do is equally complex and challenging.

This approach of examining economies as complex systems covers a lot of territory. This book covers a number of those topics, some in more depth than others. It is not meant to be a book that gives a complete picture of the global economy, but we will introduce several concepts that will hopefully give the reader a feel for the complexity of economies in the world today.

You will note that I use the metaphor of the sand pile in many parts of the book. I borrowed the idea from Joshua Cooper Ramo's book *The Age of the Unthinkable,* which helped put a context to my thinking. The sand pile seemed like a perfect tool to help explain the complexity of the world in which we live. I have used the idea of Ramo's sand pile in speeches and lectures, carefully giving him credit, and it has seemed to help people grasp many otherwise confusing concepts. Ramo's book is not about economics, as most of the books in the bibliography are, but his, like the others, was of great help as I tried to make sense of the economic twists and turns we've experienced over the past several years. Thus, it should be clear that any errors in the interpretation of data, information, or reasoning are solely mine.

Mark L. Akers
Indianapolis, Indiana
July 2013

CHAPTER 1

BRIEFLY, THE LONG-TERM SAND PILE

The future is already here—it's just not evenly distributed.

—William Gibson, The Economist, December 4, 2003

Since the beginning of the human presence on Earth, we have sought after more. Not only is having more a good thing, it seems to be important to many of us to have more than others. The desire to have more is a theme in countless stories, plays, movies, and literature from all cultures and is played out in our politics. For many, having more has become the measure of self-worth and of success or failure in life. The desire to have more is also the basis for most of our economies. Although many of us found Gordon Gekko, Michael Douglas's character in the movie *Wall Street,* to be rather slimy, many people secretly found some truth in his statement that "greed is good." In fact, it is another way of acknowledging that Adam Smith was onto something when he described the free market in his famous book *An Inquiry into the Nature and Causes of the Wealth of Nations*, published in 1776, during a time of massive changes in economic and political thinking worldwide. Within a span of a few years, not only did the Americans declare their independence from Great Britain (1776) and actually gain it (1781) after the Revolutionary War, but the French Revolution began (1789).

This period is called the "age of enlightenment" and included new inventions that spurred the industrial revolution: the steam engine, the flying shuttle in weaving machines, and improvements in ship navigation in such technologies as the sextant. Not only were the governing systems of nations changing and economies developing market economies, but these new technologies allowed for more efficient production of goods and the ability to ship those goods to new markets overseas in steel ships powered by steam rather than wooden ships powered by wind—ships that could more quickly navigate directly to ports where the goods could be unloaded and distributed more quickly to customers. Together, these new technologies and changes in economies set the stage for forms of government controlled by the people—popular sovereignty—and ushered in the age of European dominance of the world so that by 1914, European countries controlled 85% of the land in the world, much of it for economic purposes.

By then, we were headed toward the depths of World War I, which destroyed many of the industrial and economic resources of Europe. The Treaty of Versailles put such a stranglehold on Germany that we can easily trace the treaty's effects to the rise of Adolf Hitler and the even worse destruction of World War II. In the time between the wars, we had a debt-fueled Great Depression with massive unemployment, a Dust Bowl, and poverty that brought Franklin Roosevelt to office and the New Deal programs to help cities, the unemployed, and the aged. The depression was not really erased by the New Deal but more by the spending related to World War II. When the war ended in 1945, we saw the beginning of a postwar economic expansion fueled in some ways by the new technologies developed during the war as well as by a pent-up demand for goods and services in the United States, the only real economy left standing, that lasted well into the 1960s and influenced even our current economies.

Through all these economic ups and downs, we saw the cycles of economic expansion and recession. Governments slowly developed more accurate means of gathering information about their economies and could more clearly define the beginnings and endings of these cycles—at least after the cycles had passed—and the debates in- and outside government began to focus on what role government should play in the economy, a debate that still rages today. With our ability to gather more and better information, we now can more easily identify the economic cycles that occur from time to time; however, this availability of information can fuel a mistaken belief that we have better ideas about the causes of economic cycles and what, if anything, to do about them. As with most other problems in life, it's important to know the causes in order to apply the right cures. Likewise, over time, as we have learned more and have had experience in more kinds of problems, we have often found how much we really didn't know and how wrong we can be.

THE SAND PILE AND THE MASH-UP

A few years ago, Joshua Cooper Ramo wrote a very interesting book titled *The Age of the Unthinkable*. One of the book's themes is that the world is changing so quickly that events once considered impossible or unthinkable are now occurring with some regularity and that many events that have not occurred yet must be considered inevitable. For illustration, Ramo tells of an experiment involving the structure and inner workings of a sand pile.

In 1987, a physicist named Per Bak wrote a paper in which he coined the phrase "self-organized criticality." The term referred to the state toward which a pile of sand moves as it increases in size. Basically, as the sand pile gets larger, say, than a fist, it appears to be stable but in fact is on the edge of collapse, technically called a critical state or criticality. At that point, adding just one more grain of sand may cause an avalanche on some portion of the sand pile, or it may not. It is impossible to know. Bak believed that the way the particles develop and release energy in a system such as a sand pile was a fundamental force of nature seen in such things as hard-to-predict rainstorms; however, Bak died in 2002 at the age of fifty-four and never ran an experiment to find just when criticality was reached in the sand pile. Systems such as sand piles are called "nonlinear" because they are, by nature, unpredictable and we thus cannot say that doing a certain thing to the system will result in a specific reaction. A sand pile is a "complex system" and is therefore unpredictable and nonlinear. Thus, if we can find a way to model such a system to show how it will react over a long time, physicists and even economists could possibly find how the system evolved to its present state and how it will change in the future; that's just the kind of knowledge an economist would love to have to understand how we got to where we are and what to do to produce or prolong an economic expansion.

Glenn Held is an experimental scientist and decided to do the experiment suggested by Bak, so he developed the mechanisms required to drop grains of sand, one at a time, onto a surface under controlled conditions and to see how many grains of sand it would take before the sand pile experienced an avalanche. Just as Bak had predicted, the sand self-organized into a pile without anything "telling" it to do so. It did not just fall onto the surface and spray all over in a flat random manner but eventually reached a level of criticality. Held performed the experiment several times. The first time the critical state was reached, the additional grain of sand caused a small avalanche on one side if the sand pile. In subsequent trials, however, he could add thousands of grains more to the pile before the avalanche occurred, and sometimes, it took fewer grains. Each time he ran the experiment, a different number of sand grains set off the avalanche. There were also differences in the size and placement of each collapse.

The key to what was observed was not so much in the number of grains of sand involved but in what was happening *within* the sand pile; the shifting and sliding of the grains of sand were the key to understanding how the sand pile changed. There was no specific link between how the sand pile was hit or how often and how it reacted. In fact, each time a grain of sand hit the pile, the grains in the pile all shifted slightly and created, in essence, a new pile of sand different than the one that had existed before the new grain was added. The "new" sand pile would thus react differently to the next grain that hit it than the "previous" pile would have reacted. You could say the sand pile adapted with each new hit.

Held wondered if he could model this kind of complex system, but it proved too complicated because there was no way to predict what the new pile would look like as the grains shifted and slid to new positions after each hit. Like snowflakes, no two grains of sand are alike, and the reactions of two successive piles could not be predicted. Although the movements of the grains of sand in the pile seemed like unpredictable randomness, they really weren't. It's just that we don't have the tools and the information needed to make the predictions. The behavior of the pile appears random and chaotic only because we haven't figured it out yet. It's always been that way. As Ramo put it in his book, "The logic of the world, even while expressing an immense inner order, would continue to appear to us as a senseless riot."

THE LIST

Although there is plenty of disagreement over what makes a country successful, today, most will agree that the stability and steady growth of the economy are certainly part of the mix. Fareed Zakaria in his book *The Post-American World* runs through many markers of economic prosperity that used to be dominated by the United States but that are now spread throughout the world—the world's tallest building, the world's richest man, the largest publicly traded company, the most richly endowed investment fund, and so on. His point is that the rest of the world is now prospering, not only economically but also in quality-of-life measures. Zakaria also points out that ours is also the most peaceful time in human history. To be sure, we live in a time of rapid change that comes with fighting and local conflicts. Even so, organized violence has decreased dramatically over the past two decades to the point that the University of Maryland's Center for International Development and Conflict Management concluded that "the general magnitude of global warfare has decreased...falling by 2004 to its lowest level since the late 1950s."

Why did this happen in spite of the Vietnam conflict; the fall of the Soviet Union; conflicts in and around Israel; the September 11 attacks; wars involving Kuwait, Afghanistan, and Iraq; and the Great Recession? It seems as though economic growth has occurred in the face of political upheaval.

In China, I teach a class titled Comparative Economics. In the class, we examine a number of economic systems from ancient Rome in about 50 BCE to modern China. The point of the course is to find factors that are common to countries that are doing well regardless of their forms of government and rule-making. Thus, we can say that regardless of the form of government, or even the culture or the time in history, if these things are present, countries seem to do well. Much of what is on the list is not surprising, though one or two things are. Here's the list:

A stable and competent political structure

A system for establishing rules; rules for the kinds of work that are done, who can do the work, and fairness in the way business is conducted; and the ability to enforce the rules

Social stability—a general lack of revolution, war, or serious social upheaval

Markets and competition

The presence of foreigners who are accepted and integrated into the economic and social fabric

A willingness to try new ideas

A system of welfare for those who need help

A culture that encourages ethical behavior

The more of these a nation has, the stronger these factors are, and the more they are part of the nation's history and culture, the more successful the nation will be economically and socially. Some of these items were more important in some cultures than others; some were more modern additions. To be indicators of success, these characteristics must come from within, not from without; they need to evolve as part of the society and not because a government or king decided that they were necessary.

For example, just before the fall of the Soviet Union, Mikhail Gorbachev tried to open the Soviet Union to the world and establish a market economy; however, there had been no real markets in that society since the 1917 communist revolution that brought Vladimir Lenin to power. Thus, the people in the USSR had long forgotten how to compete and how to develop new technologies and efficiencies. The government had no knowledge of how to manage a market economy and its money supply; thus, the factors of production were never able to produce products at a competitive price, and there was no real ability to market the products anyway. After Gorbechev's efforts failed and the Soviet Union fell apart, and with the unusual leadership of Boris Yeltsin, Russia eventually went back toward a stronger central government while trying to maintain some aspects of a market economic system under Vladimir Putin, a compromise that fit better with what the people were used to.

In China, after Mao died in 1976, Deng Xiaoping was able to make the transition to a market economy work by making changes slowly, allowing people to adjust and learn how to compete. The slower pace of change also allowed the factors of production to modernize: companies were able to modernize their out-of-date machines, workers could learn new skills, and companies could learn the lessons needed to compete in a market system. China really didn't get into the swing of things until the 1980s, but by the year 2000, they had enough momentum that the system so far has lifted more than 400 million people out of poverty in the last thirty years.

The items on the list above were present in all cultures that were doing well, regardless of the form of government, the dominant religious beliefs, or the culture. The government could be a strong, centrally controlled system or a democracy, there could be a dominant religion or none at all, and there could have been strong or weak cultural norms. If the items on the list were present, the economy performed well. Here, I emphasize an important point we previouly discussed: The items on the list could not be imposed by a leader or leaders but had to evolve from the history and practices of the people in the country. This usually happened when government played a lesser role, as in a democracy, rather than a stronger role, as in a dictatorship, in the social and economic lives of people. This doesn't mean government played no role. Government played a role in many items on the list; note number seven, about welfare. Foreigners are part of the country as a result of immigration and travel, and working rules and fair play are basically defined by a government made up of people who come from the culture of the immigrants' adopted country. The presence of markets, however, implies that governments are less in control of economies than they are in a classical communist system.

For several reasons, I usually discuss the list with some trepidation, especially among friends or in presentations I give to various public groups. Among the reasons for this is that some people want to use the list to show how their political views are correct and their opposition is obviously wrong, which is called a "confirmation bias." Another reason is that some want to use the list as a basis for predicting whether a nation or some part of the world will have economic growth, especially over the long term. In their zeal, both groups feel self-satisfied. In reality, they will be disillusioned.

Economic predictions have become all the rage in some circles. With the improvement in our ways of measuring economic activities and our perceived abilities to make predictions of all kinds, from weather to next week's sports scores, we are becoming overconfident in our ability to see into the economic future. A current example revolves around the growing interest in investing in emerging countries—poor countries with GDP per capita of less than $25,000 or so, but many of which are showing signs of economic growth. Some potential investors will look at the items on my list, or on similar lists, as a basis for predicting the future success of these emerging nations. Ruchir Sharma, the managing director of the Emerging Market Equity team at Morgan Stanley, has his own list in his book, *Breakout Nations: In Search of the Next Economic Miracle*. From his experience he looks at "per-capita income level, the top-ten billionaire lists, speeches of radical politicians, the prices of black-market money changers, the travel of local businessmen (whether they are moving money home or offshore), the profit margins of big monopolies, and the size of second cities (oversized capital cities often indicate excessive power in the hands of the political elite)" (p. 13).

The tendency for most people is to look at long-term predictions. By long term, I mean twenty, thirty, or maybe forty years into the future. Even if the specifics don't turn out to be very accurate, the thinking is that the overall long-term trends are pointing in the right direction—upward.

If we look at the long term, however, some issues emerge that make the usefulness of forecasts nonsense. If we're talking twenty-year predictions, we're looking only at business cycles—the time between the peak (the high point) of one economic expansion and the peak of the next. A lot happens during the expansion phase of these cycles that changes the look of the next downturn. For example, there will almost certainly be new technologies that not only affect production, medical science, and so forth, but that also affect communications. These will change the speed of contagion, change the spread of economic booms and busts, and make the economic system more complex in ways that are unpredictable. In twenty years, governments change, bringing new leaders with their new agendas and styles. In a later chapter, we will look at how these changes spread. Here, it is enough to say that "big things have small beginnings," to steal a line from Lawrence of Arabia.

Even the ability of governments to affect their economies has changed over the years. Until the industrial revolution, many economies were based on agriculture and the farms were widely dispersed and had little contact with each other, let alone with any government. Even communication of the things government was doing was rare and often incomplete or incorrect, so government policies had little to no effect on these rural economies. Of course, that has changed as time has passed. Technology changed during the buildup to the industrial revolution as water transportation improved travel by using rivers and lakes. Canals and eventually railroads were built that allowed farmers to sell their grain farther away because they could move it a greater distance before it spoiled. That also meant that communication was faster and that what was going on in the state and provincial capitals could be known by more people. Then along came the telegraph, steam engine, and iron-hulled ships that made for many forms of rapid transport and communication. When the telephone came into widespread use, everything changed again. The story of innovation in technology is near the heart of the story of economic growth throughout the world. To grow an economy, people have to make new products or have to make existing products more quickly and more cheaply. If that does not happen, the same things are stuck being made in the same way, and nothing can change or grow.

What technology growth also does is change the way people think. With faster communication over wider areas, new ideas flow everywhere very quickly. That changes what people think, the way they think, and how much they know. That's education. When people connect with others they haven't known before, it changes everything.

Today we take for granted technologies that were revolutionary when they were first introduced. The clock made time uniform over large areas that improved productivity rather than requiring that people depend on the sun or moon and the seasons. Using the telescope as part of the sextant allowed a ship to navigate directly toward their intended port instead of hitting shoreline somewhere and then searching up and down the coast for its destination. Steam power was first invented by Robert Fulton to be used in mining but later spread to agriculture, which resulted in more food being produced by fewer people. The people who left the farms went to cities, where workers were needed in a new form of production—factories—where more products were produced to satisfy all manner of life's needs and desires.

Change brings resistance to change, however. Eight decades before Columbus set sail, Zheng He sailed from China with more, bigger, and better ships than Columbus had. His first trip included more than 300 ships and 25,000 men. In all, he made seven trips into the Indian Ocean and areas around Southeast Asia, collecting many strange items, plants, and animals. He encountered many new cultures and people. In 1423, however, a new emperor, Zhu Gaochi, came to power, and after Zheng He died, the emperor decided to end the explorations and had all oceangoing ships burned. By the 1600s, the isolationist policy continued as the Qing dynasty scorched 700 miles of China's coast, making it uninhabitable and unusable for ports. It wasn't until the early 1700s that a Chinese ship made it to Europe. Government matters. Columbus sailed as China turned inward, and things changed forever. The 1800s became the European century.

In their book *Why Nations Fail,* Daron Acemoglu and James Robinson focus on the institutions that develop in various nations and cultures. Institutions here refers not only to the various forms and functions of governments but also to the ways the private sectors do business; how education systems work; the causes or impediments to innovation that may be legal, regulatory, or cultural; and related factors. They point out that where markets develop, various degrees of prosperity and personal freedoms most often are as well. The freer the markets, generally, the more prosperity and personal freedoms are seen; however, it is difficult for governments to keep their hands off of free markets or free societies. History has many examples of what can happen without some level of government regulation and enforcement. As we have seen throughout much of history, in most countries, the pendulum swings from times of relatively little government interference to times of greater government involvement, sometimes as the result of elections and the demands of the population, and sometimes because of the decisions made by strong political authorities.

We saw such a transition perhaps happen in November of 2012 in China as the Communist Party of China's national congress meeting made much of the movement for transparency, getting more serious about government corruption, and even openly discussing various forms of elections in a one-party system. If those discussions really happen, and if the rules really are changed, it could affect the way many countries do business not only with China but also with other nations and domestically as competition with Chinese companies changes and as the "soft power" discussions about the way people live in various countries ratchets up.

As we will see later when we discuss complex systems in greater detail, it's difficult to know what such changes will bring; how the sand pile will change. The changes will almost certainly result in some unintended surprises, both good and bad. We can assume, however, that there will be a change in the economic games that nations must play if the effects of China's changes are real and perhaps significant. As nations try to anticipate these changes and react to them, there will be more unexpected outcomes, things we cannot predict today. That's one of the characteristics of complex systems: they try to adapt. Sometimes they adapt with ease, but most often, they don't, especially when politics is involved. The implications for long-term predictions and for making public policy in such a world are that each nation, within its own culture and with its own institutions, will try to make adjustments, making many misjudgments because of the systems it has for making policy as well as because of its incomplete information. Each nation will also make mistakes because it has a population that is less informed than its leaders, but a population that still makes demands for change.

So, what do these decisions affect? What are the limits of these effects? Why can't politicians ever get it right?

CHAPTER 2

GDP

> I always avoid prophesying beforehand because it is much better to prophesy after the event has already taken place.
>
> —Winston Churchill

If we are going to show how complexity affects our ability to understand how economies work, it is useful to understand how nations currently look at economies. The current method is pretty straightforward in that it categorizes different economic activities and adds them together. When we use such a method, however, the results we get—and the predictions we make—can end up being very different from what is actually happening or can end up occurring in the future.

Until 1991, the US government used gross national product (GNP) as the primary measure of economic activity. It switched to the gross domestic product (GDP) for two primary reasons. First, GNP is a measure of the market value of the final goods and services produced by a county's enterprises, whether the enterprises are located inside the country or not. By contrast, GDP is the market value of all final goods and services produced *within* the country, whether produced by domestic or foreign firms. In making the change, the Bureau of Economic Analysis (BEA) said that GDP made comparisons of the components of overall economic activity in the country much easier. Second, most other countries had already adopted GDP as their primary measure of economic activity.

Let's examine GDP in more detail. Gross domestic product is the market value of all final goods and services produced by a country during a given period, usually one year. Thus, because GDP is the market value of those goods and services, it includes only those items that are bought and sold in the marketplace of normal commerce and does not include those things sold privately between individuals, such as a person selling his old lawn mower to his neighbor. The term "final goods and services" means that GDP includes only those things that are sold to the final user of those items, the people or companies that use the end product, so the customer who buys a tire sold at a tire store, puts it on his car, and drives away is the final consumer of the value of the tire, and the sale is included in GDP. However, if the tire is sold by the manufacturer to an auto company that makes cars and the tire is put onto a car in the production process, it is not included in GDP because the car company is not the final user of the tire. The value of that tire is included in the cost of the car and is added to GDP only when the car is sold.

In addition, only new goods and services that are produced and sold in the year being measured are included. GDP for this year does not include unsold goods produced last year. Used cars or existing homes are not included because they were produced and sold in previous years and have already been counted in that year's GDP.

If you think about it, you realize that if a product is sold, it produces income for the seller. Thus, GDP also works as a measure of total income for the year.

THE COMPONENTS OF GDP

Goods and services included in GDP are sold to three groups: domestic households (Consumption), foreign companies and households (Net Exports), and government (Government Spending). More specifically, the goods and services sold to domestic households are the products that consumers buy for their own use throughout the year. The Government Spending category of GDP is made up mostly of the goods and services that government buys as well as the money that government transfers to others without getting anything in return (Social Security, welfare, etc.). The sale of goods and services to foreign companies and households (which brings money into the United States) constitutes exports. If we subtract from exports the sale of goods from foreign companies to US consumers (which sends money out of the United States), we get a number for the Net Exports category of GDP.

Now, if you and I earn more money than we spend, what we don't spend is our savings. Savings are most often held in various forms in financial institutions, which use the money for lending. We borrow when we spend more money than we make. When households, companies, and others need to upgrade or buy new machines, factories, or houses, for example, they usually borrow to do so. Financial institutions can't loan money unless they have it, and thus the money they have to loan is close to the amount we save, so it turns out that the amount of savings of all kind is equal to the Investment category of GDP because the Investment category is the amount that households and businesses invest in plants and equipment, houses, and similar assets.

There are thus four components of GDP: consumption of goods and services by domestic households, investments made by companies using the savings we have in financial institutions, government spending, and the difference between imports and exports, called net exports. If we say that "Y" represents GDP, we can show how GDP works with a simple formula: Y = C + I + G +NX.

Although this is a mathematical formula, it's pretty easy to figure out. It says that our GDP, Y, is made up of Consumption (C), Investment (I), Government Spending (G), and Net Exports (NX). When we add all those things together, C + I + G + NX, we get GDP. The largest portion of GDP in the United States is, by far, consumption (C), which is consumer spending, or what you and I buy. It makes up about 70% of the US GDP, so if we don't spend, GDP takes a big hit. If we do spend, GDP most often increases. Investment (I) is the spending of companies on factories, land, and equipment. As we imply above, companies can't invest as much if we don't save money, because companies normally have to borrow money to expand, and banks can't loan money unless they have it. Savings is defined as the amount of income we don't spend.

Let's discuss savings a little more. Total savings come from two sources: private-sector savings (you and me and companies) and public savings from government. Government has income, too, in the form of taxes. If the government spends less than it gets in taxes, it has a surplus, which means it has savings—it's spending less than it makes. If it spends more than it gets in taxes, it has a deficit and, like you and me and companies, it has to borrow. It borrows by selling government bonds. What a deficit does, then, is reduce total savings and increase the borrowing of the money that the banks have left from the reduced private savings. Because there is only a certain amount available from private saving—there is a limit to what we can save. If government borrowing goes up because of a deficit, it can "crowd out" private borrowing and reduce the amount of money available for investment in building, machines, and houses—the "I" category of GDP. Although we can currently handle the cost of the government deficit because the interest rates on government bonds are near zero, the government deficit still reduces the private-sector ability to invest in productive assets and to grow GDP.

Net exports (NX) is the money we get by exporting minus the money we have to pay to others when we import. Thus, if we export more than we import, we have a trade surplus and money comes into the United States. If we import more than we export, money flows out of the United States and we have a trade deficit. If we export more than we import, money comes in and helps GDP increase. GDP is hurt when we import more than we export.

This formula for GDP is at work in all economies, regardless of whether they are controlled by a democratic republic (the United States) or a dictatorship (North Korea). The way governments operate and set the rules of commerce will affect the emphasis placed on each category. For example, much of the tremendous growth of China's economy has been fueled by enormous expenditures on the nation's infrastructure—government spending (G) and exports (NX). In the United States, the growth is fueled by consumer spending (C). You might notice that consumer spending, investment, and net exports are all functions that happen in markets—supply and demand. Government spending, however, is not; it results from political decisions. Government decides when to spend and not to spend, but only partly in response to market forces; thus, if consumption is down, companies aren't investing, and we have a trade deficit (all of which occurred in the 2007–2009 recession), government spending is the only category left to increase GDP. If government decreases spending in a time of falling GDP, it will make the recession worse. If the government increases spending, it can keep GDP from falling into recession, lessen the severity of the recession, or perhaps help start an expansion. Thus, government spending provides a tool to help stimulate or slow the economy. At least that's the theory. Politics, however, often get in the way of sound decisions about the policies and programs that should be put into place to make the economy stronger. In the case of China, the government's political decision to control the value of its currency, the yuan, compared to the US dollar also affects net exports. With the value of the yuan lower than the *market* price would be, Chinese-made products are cheaper in the market than US products are. Thus, China exports more than it would if the government let the yuan float to its market value. China feels a need to do this because so many Chinese citizens are moving to cities and it would be a disaster to have tens of millions of unemployed people move into cities so quickly, so the nation exports to create jobs. In this case, a political decision is used in an attempt to affect a market factor. A few other poor countries are trying to do the same thing.

The twentieth century became the American century. More than a decade into the twenty-first century, there's still a lively argument going on as to whether this will be the Asian century. Why? The rules are changing. It used to be relatively clear that if economic growth was measured by GDP, the United States had a healthy, sustained growth for much of the twentieth century. Now, however, the rules regarding how we measure economic, military, and soft power are being challenged by the tremendous growth of China. China now has the second largest GDP on the planet, and some predictions suggest that China may catch the United States over the next decade or so (a long-term forecast). By the rules for measuring economic strength, however, China is still a poor nation, fitting into the category of an emerging country. US GDP per capita is approaching $49,000 per year. China's is approaching $6,000. China has a land mass similar to that of the United States, but instead of 300 million people, China has more than 1.3 billion people. It takes a lot more GDP to supply the needs of 1.3 billion than it does to supply the needs of the 0.3 billion in the United States. GDP grows much faster in China than in the United States (7% to 9% for China, 2% to 3% for the United States) for many reasons: wages and productivity of labor, internal control of interest rates, and China's control of its currency exchange rate. As of this writing, China's GDP is a little more than half that of the United States ($8.5 trillion compared to $16.1 trillion). On average, at current rates of growth, China grows about $200 million a year faster than the United States does. Will that continue? It will take a long-term forecast to guess. China's growth in 2012 was slowing. Wages are increasing, and the nation is fighting a low-grade inflation by slowing government spending while cities are dealing with population growth (more than 50% of Chinese now live in cities), which will slow the economy more. The United States is showing slow growth in GDP, being hampered by China's slowing growth and the debt crises in Europe.

If we use the definition of an emerging nation as a nation having a GDP of less than $25,000 or so, China is an emerging nation. Although its growth has been very impressive, the other nations in this category have also been doing well. As Ruchir Sharma reported, between 2003 and 2007, the average annual GDP growth of 180 of the 183 emerging nations almost doubled (from 3.6% to 7.2%), 114 of them at more than 5%. We may look at the lists of things that are present when economic growth happens in countries, which we discussed in Chapter 1, and assume that some combination of these lined up in just the right way for these 180 countries. At the same time, some emerging nations did make positive policy choices. In the years between 2003 and 2007, a flood of money was roaming the world, looking for a place to land. There was so much money that it caused the housing bubble in the United States that burst in 2008, a central factor in creating the Great Recession. This roaming money did, however, land in many emerging countries that it had skipped over before.

Part of the problem today is that while central banks are still putting money into their economies to try to jump-start them, there is less demand for products as consumers reduce their debt rather than accumulate more. Thus, the money is not going into production and into investments such as factories. China and other emerging nations are fighting various levels of inflation rather than building infrastructure, education systems, and improved factories. Because they're not putting money into productivity, but into fighting inflation instead, it takes more debt to produce every dollar of additional GDP. So, with all this going on and likely to continue for some time, you tell me: what's the forecast for the next twenty years?

Much of economic theory and practice is based on the assumption that people are rational—that they make decisions based on gathering information, analyzing it, and making choices based on their analysis. I know a few people who believe they use such a process. Even if they do (I doubt it), they are the exceptions. The decisions that people make about what clothes to buy, what kind and how much food to eat, which job to take, and just about every other issue in life are rarely based solely on logic and reason. Decisions are most often based on incomplete information analyzed through the lens of emotion, passion, desire to be accepted by others, and some short-term situational pressures. On top of all that, we don't even decide what price we will we pay for any given purchase. We usually have to either take or leave the price on a price tag put there by the seller. We don't bid or negotiate. We really don't know as much about the quality of the product as the seller knows, what it is made of, and sometimes why we even need to buy it (everyone else has one; I'll start my diet tomorrow; this one is better than my neighbor's). How much rationalizing can go into a purchase or just walking away?

Large corporations and financial institutions move enormous amounts of money around the world—about $2 trillion each day. Even so, at the heart and soul of this movement of money is the sale of products and services to consumers—you and me. The economic cycle works like this: We make the products that companies sell; we provide the services that companies decided to render; they pay us to do that work; we spend our paychecks on the goods we made and use many of the services we render.

Government and contributions to religious organizations and charities take some money out of the cycle and put a wide variety of services back in, but without this economic cycle, nothing gets made, taxes don't get paid, and contributions to charities don't happen. That's why unemployment hurts so much: people don't have money to spend, so companies don't make products to sell. To the degree that people don't have jobs, the economic cycle is broken.

One role of government in this system is to set the rules of fair play. This includes such things as laws regarding the enforcement of contracts, protection of intellectual property, and ethics, such as truth in advertising and product safety. Included are also the laws and policies regarding how interstate and international business is conducted. In this system, government also establishes those government agencies that are required to monitor, enforce, and supply the needs of business—infrastructure, public safety, and an independent central bank and judiciary, among other services. Companies compete for our business, hoping we'll buy the stuff we made with the money they paid us. This economic cycle is basically stable, but it can be thrown out of balance by government policies or world economic conditions. When that happens, it often takes other government policies to get things going again.

By and large, government doesn't produce many physical goods. If it wants to build roads, schools, or fire stations or to buy uniforms, for example, it hires companies in the private sector to do the work. This outsourcing is becoming a larger and larger part of government spending in every nation. Thus, after we pay taxes, some of it comes back in the form of government spending—not as efficiently as if it had been left in the private sector, but some of it does come back. Government is a consumer, too.

When we start thinking about making forecasts, then, we are looking at four issues: consumption, investment, government spending, and net exports. When we look at government economic and fiscal policies (taxing and spending), the effects on these four issues tell us a lot about what will happen in the economy. For example, when the economy is slow, consumption and investment are usually slow as well. If the market isn't ready to bring them back up to acceptable levels, government often steps in and makes a political decision to increase government spending by building roads or schools, by providing more scholarships for students, and by providing other public services. The government uses private companies and people to do most of this, and when those companies and people are paid, they spend their money (consumption) and, according to this equation, the economy improves. When consumption is too high and inflation is a danger, government spending can be slowed; without as much government spending, overall spending slows and reduces the threat of inflation, again according to the equation. In fact, it does work that way sometimes.

Changes in the level of GDP often come in cycles, sometimes called business cycles. When GDP increases, we experience economic expansion. When GDP declines, we experience recession. At the highest point in an expansion, we have reached the *peak* of the cycle. At the lowest point in the GDP cycle, we have reached the *trough*. The duration of the business cycle is usually measured from peak to peak. The problem, of course, is that while we are in the cycle, we can't tell if we are at the peak or trough, or even how close we are to either. Because government tries to stimulate the economy in a recession so it will go into an expansion, government has to know if we are still actually in a recession or if we have passed the trough and are on our way up in an expansion. Stimulating an expanding economy can cause inflation, so knowing where we are in a business cycle has important implications for government policy. Likewise, if the government tries to slow the economy because of a fear of inflation, it needs to know if the economy is still in an expansion or has passed the peak and begun a recession. Slowing an economy in recession will deepen the downturn.

The reason it is sometimes so difficult to know where we are in a business cycle is that it takes several weeks to gather the economic data from all the parts of the economy and then tabulate it and make any needed adjustments. When the data is finally available, it still has to be interpreted as part of a trend up or down or as an aberration—a smaller trend within a longer trend that is headed in the other direction. Then, if government decides what policy is needed, it takes time to implement that policy, and it takes even more time before the policy can affect the economy once implemented. You can see how making a mistake in making the correct economic policy is a real possibility, even a likelihood. These pitfalls also provide the energy for regular and constant political arguments between those who want more government involvement in the economy and those who want less. Business cycles are also near the heart of this book's discussion: how they work, what causes them, and whether we can make predictions about them.

The problem is that the economy is so complex that no equations or formulas always describe what will result from changes in consumption, investment, government spending, or net exports, or all of them together. Why? First, no one national economy is an island. Most of the 193 countries of the world (if you include the Vatican) are tied together to varying degrees, and what happens in one can affect what happens in others. The United States cannot control changes in China, Europe, or anywhere else, yet those changes have a direct effect on the level of America's GDP. The political decision of China to control the value of its currency is a good example of other economies affecting the US economy. Second, economies are made up of people, and their reactions, decisions, new ideas, and innovations are always surprising. Third, improvement still needs to be made in our ability to collect information that tells us what the economy is doing, not just in the United States, but also in China, Europe, Canada, Mexico, Russia, and most everywhere Americans do business. Not only is information collected differently in different countries, but some countries are just better at it than others. Still, there are other countries that put a political spin on their data for their own purposes, and some don't collect certain information at all. To compare the GDP of the United States with that of another country isn't always a truly valid comparison because the numbers that go into the calculations of the two GDPs are different.

When we make GDP comparisons with emerging countries, the problem is worse. Many emerging countries are small and either have a history of corruption or lack enough people with the expertise or ability to collect and interpret national information. Thus, we come back to the question about just how good a forecast, especially one that goes out twenty years or more, is when it is based on who knows what kind of information.

CHAPTER 3

WHY ARE SOME COUNTRIES SO POOR AND OTHERS SO RICH?

In a country well governed, poverty is something to be ashamed of.
In a country badly governed, wealth is something to be ashamed of.

Confucius

With the background in measuring economic activity that we gained in the first two chapters, let's now begin to see why we need to look at more than just the components of GDP if we are to understand how economies work in the real world. This chapter will begin to explain what a complex system is and how that concept applies to economies.

Why are some countries so poor and others so rich? Why have most of poor nations been poor for centuries, passed by the economic expansion that has engulfed much of the world in the last twenty or so years? Many commentators and writers have suggested that it has to do with lack of natural resources, poor infrastructure, lack of education, or dictatorial political systems that are as corrupt as they are inept. Although many of those factors apply in poor countries, in my experience, they are symptoms that magnify the real causes—history (especially political history) and cultures that evolve over hundreds of years as a result of that history.

In the 1980s, I was in charge of Indiana's economic and industrial development programs. Our goal was to attract new companies to Indiana to build factories and create jobs. We also wanted existing Indiana companies to modernize or expand in order to keep the jobs already in existence and add to the existing base. To accomplish those goals, we had to change our cities and towns not only with regard to their infrastructure but also with regard to the lifestyles they offered.

Thus, like every other state, Indiana engaged in stiff competition for jobs and investment, but the competition was especially heated between Indiana and its surrounding states. In those days, northern Indiana had the most success in attracting new companies because Michigan had much higher taxes and utility and other costs for businesses, including workers compensation for injured workers and unemployment compensation for laid-off workers, so many companies in southern Michigan moved across the border into Indiana, kept most of their workers, served the same markets, and cut their costs of doing business. As part of my job, I gave many speeches in both Indiana and Michigan to business and community groups. In one part of my talks, I often noted that when I fly in an airplane across the border between Indiana and Michigan, I see nothing to indicate I've crossed into another state. There are no fences, and the ground outside my window doesn't change color; it all looks the same. I observed, however, that as I cross the state line, people on one side of my airplane do things that people on the other side of the airplane are not doing—they are working, they buy more things because they have more money in their pockets, they live in houses that are a little nicer, and their children wear clothes that are just a little nicer. Why? Because on the Indiana side of my airplane, they have lower costs, less government regulation, and lower cost for the things they buy. In the 1980s, a border county in Michigan even wanted to secede from Michigan and join Indiana. Over the years, both Michigan and Indiana have changed, and now the competition is very close.

As the years passed and I studied economics and public policy, I found that there was actually more to that observation about the differences in Michigan and Indiana than I had considered in my speech. There was history.

Economics is a behavioral science. It studies how people behave with their money, so when I studied economics, I not only learned the theories of Adam Smith, John Maynard Keynes, and others but also studied how people behave and why. In some ways, studying how people behave with money was like following Alice down the rabbit hole: A lot of things were surprising, and many were very strange. If one goal of economics is to describe how people are behaving with money, then another goal is to try to predict what they will do with their money so economists can suggest to government what to do to make the economy work better. The Bureau of Labor Statistics says that in 2008, there were approximately 14,800 economists in the United States. Thus, on any economic subject, there are close to 14,800 opinions on what is happening and what will happen next. If we have theories from some of the great minds of our time, and if we have the technology to develop very accurate information, why can't we come closer to either agreement or accuracy? Well, it's historically complex. Literally.

Without realizing it, most of us behave the way we do, believe the things we do, and even build and decorate the way we do largely because it's the way our ancestors behaved, believed, built, and decorated perhaps hundreds of years ago. Our history is the major determinant of how we behave and think about the world around us. Our culture was set long before we were born. Here's a quick example: Today, about 7,000 active languages are spoken in the world. Those languages are clustered in different geographic areas. With global travel and communications systems, some languages have become more dominant; however, even where there are several languages now spoken, there is a native tongue. China, for example, has more English-speaking people than does the United States—more than 300 million—but it has more than a billion people who speak only Chinese. There are even a number of dialects of Chinese spoken in different parts of the country. The dominant Chinese dialect is Mandarin, but Cantonese is spoken in the south and in Hong Kong. Japanese is based on Chinese but is still very different. Even some of the written symbols are the same but have different meanings in Japan than in China.

Look at the architecture of homes in Asia compared to Europe and the United States, or the methods of educating our children that bring such divergent results between nations, within nations, and even within cities. Different governmental systems are used in different parts of the world: multiparty democracies in the West, and single-party dictatorships in the Middle East and Asia, all of which have different philosophies. Dictatorships come in many forms, from the Chinese model of Communism with a market economy, to the military-controlled systems such as those in North Korea and parts of Africa. Democracies come in more socialist flavors in Europe and less socialist flavors in the United States. As with languages, governmental systems are clustered based on the histories of the development of those parts of the world. Similar examples exist with religion, which side of the road drivers use, and the most popular sports and which teams play those sports.

Recall the list that I showed earlier of things that are always present when a country is doing well. In different cultures with different histories, the items on that list persisted for very long periods of time, many until the end of those societies and governments; sometimes they were so strongly held by the culture that they caused the fall or change in direction of governments that strayed from those long-held principles. Where the items on that list work, they largely reflect the culture of the people in the styles and systems of governments.

Several theories have developed regarding why some countries flourish and others do not. Some relate the difference to geography—how far north or south of the equator the country lies, for example—and the cultures that evolve in such locations. Some suggest that the degree of economic success or failure has to do with the natural mineral or energy resources in the area, or perhaps the kinds of animals and plants indigenous to the area, saying that the ability to domesticate certain kinds of animals made the area more suitable for farming and the technology that comes with farming. There are also theories using culture as an explanation, relating a country's prosperity to the religion (Protestant work ethic, for example) or the types of secular beliefs, values, and ethics that evolved in the area (the presence of black magic, laziness of the people, or resistance to Western technology, for example). However, none of these explain how we see the vast inequalities in incomes and influence between countries and within countries that have the same or similar cultures. Almost always, the differences in beliefs, values, and ethics are a result of these inequalities, not the other way around. The former president of China, Hu Jintao, very publicly acknowledged the huge problem that its government has with corruption, saying that if China cannot control and eliminate corruption, it could cause the fall of the country's governing system. The Chinese have known for a long time that a single-party system leads to corruption, and now they are openly talking about moving toward democracy and transparency in government. Any such movement will take many years because the history of China has been of a strong central government without elections; however, the Chinese government appears to see the need for the people to trust their government. After all, the communist government in China came to power through revolution in 1949 and doesn't want to lose power in the same way. The Chinese government is committed to "socialism with Chinese characteristics" but won't jump right into elections. Its habit is to go slowly and give people and the system time to adjust. That approach is how China moved from Mao-style communism to the market system it has today—one step at a time. The government is not trying to change the culture of China. The government is going to adapt to the culture to the way the world is moving.

Let's get back to my speech about Michigan and Indiana. There are differences in the cultures and belief systems about government, unions, education, work, and even the weather, between large portions of the people of Michigan and large portions of the people in Indiana. Michigan is more urban; its cities are larger. It is more industrialized; the state has a lot more large companies. It has more corporate headquarters, more union workers, more government help for unemployed and injured workers, and more workplace safety laws, and a lot more people are Democrats in Michigan. When it's cold in Indiana, people go inside. In Michigan, they go outside to play.

By contrast, Indiana is more rural; it has only one really large city and lots of farm-based communities. Indiana has few corporate headquarters. It's a branch-plant state, so when companies make decisions about Indiana, the decisions are made by people who are someplace else and who probably know little about Indiana. Indiana has fewer large industries than Michigan, and few unions and union workers. The government runs small, with less help for unemployed and injured workers and with fewer workplace safety laws. Most people in Indiana are Republicans. Indiana has many great interstate highways but few things to attract visitors, so a lot more people have driven *through* Indiana than have driven *to* Indiana. The population in Indiana grows, but not much more than birth and death rates dictate.

Why the difference? Do these things mean Michigan is better? Of course not, but its economy is different—sometimes better than Indiana's, sometimes worse. Indiana's unemployment rate is usually the lowest in the Midwest, but that is because even though a larger portion of its workforce works in manufacturing categories, it has fewer factories and industrial workers and fewer unions. It has many factories, some of them very large, but not near as many factories as Ohio, Michigan, and Illinois. Indiana also became a right-to-work state in 2012, meaning unions can't force employees who are not part of a company union to pay dues to the union, so union influence is lower in Indiana than in Michigan. Naturally, many people in Indiana want the state to have a faster-growing economy.

Many other people like things the way they are. That's part of the culture as well. Part of the difference is the way both states were settled as the country moved west in its early days. Michigan and northern Indiana were settled from east to west as people from New England moved through the waterways and Great Lakes on their journeys. Southern Indiana, however, was settled from south to north. In those days, the southern states were slave states and the concept of work had a different meaning than it did for people from New England, who believed in hard work as a way to make a fortune (the Protestant work ethic). Today, there is still a difference between the north, which has most of the factories and economic activities of Indiana, and the south, which is more rural in spite of the poorer farmland. Even the speech patterns are different. In the southern part of Indiana, many people have a "Southern" accent similar to accents in Kentucky, Tennessee, and Georgia. The settlers had to clear the land from dense forests for farming. They did it on their own, without help from outsiders, which still describes the feelings of many rural Hoosiers about outsiders.

Although these are generalities about Indiana and Michigan, they are an accurate reflection of how countries' economies and cultures reflect their pasts. When there have been significant changes in an economy or culture, they have followed significant changes in the governing systems from one of monarchy or dictator, in which a ruling elite prospered and the population suffered, to one in which the population had significant say in the way government was run and the population prospered more than the leaders. Even China, which has a one-party system, now has a system in which the population prospers through a market-based economy, a relatively new occurrence for China. Even so, the Chinese government appears to be trying to change in response to the needs of the population, even if it's so those in government can stay in power. Political leadership responding to the needs and desires of citizens in order to stay in office is the good side of politics even in a democracy.

One effect of government responding to public needs is the development of new institutions that arise from these beginnings. The term "institutions" here means the various forms of governance that evolve from these cultural and historical differences. One country or state puts more emphasis on social programs, and the agencies, budgets, and skills of the people hired make those "institutions" different than in those countries or states that emphasize other policies. We have seen this effect over and over again throughout history. Once society starts in a given direction, the trends persist. That's why it is difficult to change the economies of countries or states and the inequalities that exist in those places. In addition, as these institutions that help the population evolve, they also benefit the politicians who control them; the institutions and the work they do are seen as good and necessary, and their political managers are seen as performing necessary jobs and thus gain, hopefully, positive notoriety.

In the United States, economic institutions allow people to start companies easily, without many barriers, and to get their financing through a variety of sources. The companies can then hire workforces trained in good schools and that make products sold and moved to buyers using well-developed transportation and communications systems. These institutions allow people to dream, to believe they can innovate without having their ideas stolen, or to at least have the opportunity to try. Once these institutions are begun, they change everything that existed before, and they last. The list of the richest fifty countries of 100 or even 150 years ago would be very similar to the same list for today. A similar list of US states would change only slightly, and most of the changes would be because a person or group living in a location lower on the list had an idea that hit it big. The heart of the early auto industry was in Indiana, but Henry Ford lived in Detroit. Bill

Gates started Microsoft in Arizona but moved it to his hometown of Seattle. There are many more examples.

Once these institutions are in place, over time, they make big differences in the economies of countries and states. Even if the cultures of two places are the same at some point, the outcomes are different. If the cultures are different at the start, the outcomes will be vastly different. In the case of North Korea and South Korea, two different sets of political institutions evolved in societies that were essentially the same, and today the difference is stark. Look at a satellite photograph of the Korean Peninsula at night. There are no lights in North Korea. South of the 38th Parallel, the lights are bright across the whole country, especially in the cities. In 1909, Europeans coming to the West had a real choice about where to go—North America or Argentina, which had different cultures but very similar economies and prospects for future growth. Over the course of the twentieth century, the institutions of North America and Argentina changed, and today, the United States has a GDP per capita nearly three times Argentina's, which is now a poor country. Within the United States, there is a large difference between Washington, DC and Delaware—which have the largest GDP per capita in the economies and prospects for their citizens' futures—as compared with Mississippi and West Virginia, which have the lowest per-capita GDPs.

If we look at the list in another 50 or 100 years, there will likely be little change. Population makes a difference in those numbers, but the million people in Delaware get a lot more out of their economy per person than the two and three million in West Virginia and Mississippi, respectively, even though all three are basically rural states. (The District of Columbia is a different animal. Although its official population is about 600,000, it draws workers from a wide area, and on any given working day, more than a million people are in town, spending their money, so DC's GDP per capita is more than double that of second-place Delaware. Washington, DC is not even a typical urban area, and comparisons with other cities and states are hard to make.) Because the size of the population can make some numbers look better or worse, even if you look at the median household incomes or personal income measures, West Virginia and Mississippi are at the bottom of the lists. History and the cultures that evolve from those histories matter a great deal.

CHAPTER 4

IT GETS COMPLEX

> An ocean traveler has even more vividly the impression that the ocean is made of waves than it is made of water.
>
> —Arthur Stanley Eddington

Now let's get specific about complex systems. They are all around us. We see them in action, and we are part of them. We most often don't notice them because they are a normal part of our daily lives. They are also what allow market economies to be so successful, as well as to falter. So, what exactly are complex adaptive systems? How do they work?

Because I am a college professor, friends and even strangers want to tell me about their opinions, something they read, or theories they have developed through observation and the input of a television or newspaper commentator. Some of these discussions have a few shreds of reason in them, but most are not well considered. If I really don't want to respond and start an argument or prolong the conversation, I'll just nod my head from time to time, make a "hmmm" sound, and try to find a way to not prolong the discussion. I don't want to offend these people, as many are good friends. Trying to convince them of another point of view is usually fruitless, however. I have found over the years that the vast majority of people really aren't aware of many facts, data, or other information that applies to their points of view; they just have points of view and have justified those views with pieces of information they have picked up along the way that they think support their theories.

The general public just doesn't grasp the workings of economies, and who can blame them? The economy is complex, multinational, and politically charged and involves topics they have never heard of. During election cycles, the public's understanding gets worse as politicians feed the public views that professional writers and consultants craft to sound right and that are backed by "theory" or "science." Such views are, however, not meant to inform the public but rather to get votes. Some time ago, I said as much in a newspaper article, presenting some facts and data to back up my position, and was accused of being both a Republican and a Democrat, too liberal and too conservative, or favoring one candidate as well as the other; no one addressed the facts, data, or reasoning that I presented. They used the same tactics that politicians use—attack the messenger rather than the message. Perhaps that's the world the public is now part of, a world largely uninformed on many topics, in which members of the public parrot what their political parties or favorite candidates say rather than try to find out who is closer to the truth or closer to an informed point of view.

George Kennan, one of the greatest Foreign Service officers and diplomats of the twentieth century, spent 1946 and 1947 at the National War College at Fort McNair in Washington, DC, lecturing and writing. During his stay, he gave a series of thirteen lectures that are now in a book titled *Measures Short of War*. Reading those lectures, you can see that he was trying to come to grips with the need for a new way of thinking after World War II and with the changes the world was facing with nuclear weapons and the new divisions of power in Europe, which was by then carved into new political pieces. Perhaps we find ourselves at a similar time, says Joshua Ramo. We have new technologies that spread ideas and the power to turn ideas into reality more quickly than ever before. Democracies are noted for being "messy" according to many, allowing their citizens the freedom to come up with their own ideas and tell as many people as they can about those ideas. Although this is a perfect environment for innovation, it is also a perfect environment for the unpredictable. With market systems spreading around the globe, the sand pile is getting larger and is growing in complexity. Devising ways to affect the sand pile socially and economically will thus require new ways of thinking.

There are too many examples of the changes from the more linear past ways of thinking and doing. Those linear ways of thinking provided great inventions and enormous growth for us and the world, but those ways are quickly slipping away. What linear thinking is now providing, says Ramo, is often the opposite of what we intend. The world has become far too complex, and the formulas we used to use to explain this new world can't account for all the new inputs required to make them work. On December 11, 1974, economist Friedrich August von Hayek delivered his Nobel lecture in Stockholm. He was one of the first to receive the prize for economics. His lecture was titled "The Pretense of Knowledge." The notion that we can treat complex topics as though they are simple, he said, is dangerous. "There is much reason to be apprehensive about the long range dangers created in a much wider field by the uncritical acceptance of assertions which have the appearance of being scientific," he said. "If man is not to do more harm than good in his efforts to improve the social order, he will have to learn that in this, as in all other fields where essential complexity of an organized kind prevails, he cannot acquire the full knowledge which would make mastery of the events possible."

COMPLEX SYSTEMS

As a beginning to this discussion, I want to introduce economist Hyman Minsky, who I learned of in Paul Krugman's book *End This Depression Now!*. Minsky taught at Washington University in St. Louis. He was not near the center of economic writings and discussions but rather on the margins and was so until his death in 1996. He proposed many theories and wrote many papers, but only a few of his predictions proved to be insightful. Part of one of his ideas, however, may apply to economic cycles: One person's debt is another person's asset. What this means is that *total* wealth is not really affected by debt, especially on a macro scale—for the world and perhaps for some large countries. In this view, an individual can go into debt to buy a house, for example, and not affect total wealth. If that person sells the house, the mortgage is paid off and things don't change much in the economy; money just changes hands in the paying off of a debt, and the total economic activity is unchanged.

What if, however, everyone sold their houses at the same time? Then we would have a problem because there are more sellers than buyers and the price—actually, the value—of the individual's house falls but the loan cannot be paid off. Then we have a true drop in wealth in the economy. Thus, those activities that we do at random do not affect total wealth much, but the activities we perform in sync can cause things to go awry. This is what happened at the beginning of the 2007–2009 recession. Many homeowners could not make their payments, the banks foreclosed, a great numbers of houses came on the market at the same time, and prices fell. It didn't help that bank foreclosures almost always mean that houses are sold for below-market prices. Who would have thought that all those people would default on their mortgages at the same time? Economist Paul Krugman called it our Minsky Moment.

We will come back to this idea of the Minsky Moment. For now, let's define what a complex system is and see how it fits into economics. Very basically, complex systems are large numbers of individual entities—people, for example—that organize themselves into a group that creates patterns of behavior, uses information, and often evolves and learns, without any central control telling the individuals to do or not do something. There are several examples in nature; Melanie Mitchell reports in her book, *Complexity: A Guided Tour,* that army ants, which are nearly blind, create specific patterns as they move from one location to another, killing and devouring prey in their path. They will use the prey's bodies as bridges when they cross gaps in their path. Another example is that of the immune system. In some animals, the immune system is made of different types of cells distributed throughout the body working together efficiently and effectively without any central control to fight disease and injuries.

Likewise, economies are complex systems. The individual entities are people and companies buying and selling goods. Their collective behavior is certainly hard to predict, as we see in various markets that you and I create—changes in prices reflecting a wide variety of causes. People also adapt on a large scale (macroeconomics) and at the local level (microeconomics) to gain more profit or avoid loss. Some economists believe that these large-scale and local markets tend to seek equilibrium in regard to supply and demand. Mitchell notes that economists have tried to use the study of complex systems to study global economic behavior such as market bubbles and crashes.

Nobel Laureate Thomas C. Schelling explores complexity in several of his writings, including *Micromotives and Macrobehavior*. He tends to examine the behavior in complex systems more than the mathematics in them. His approach is to study how people respond in an environment that consists of other people responding to *their* environments (his italics), something he calls contingent behavior. According to Schelling, with people, we are dealing with conscious decisions in pursuit of goals that are limited by the information available to those people making the decisions. In addition, people sometimes make choices that are misguided or without having goals in mind. Like many economists who have questioned Adam Smith's assumption of a rational human being, Schelling attributes some decisions and actions to our subconscious needs and desires—rational or not—which in turn will affect the decisions of others, making predicting the behavior of the whole group difficult.

Let's briefly look at the connections people have with others. Robert Putnam in *Bowling Alone* describes how people interact with each other and the importance of networks. Networks are formed with two kinds of social capital: bonding and bridging. Bonding capital is in the kind of relationships we build with family members, including our extended families that may live in other cities. Bridging reflects looser ties across extended friendships and acquaintances. When we look at the spread of ideas and innovations, it is this second type that is more important. This may seem counterintuitive, but when we think about it, we realize that we tend to have stable relationships with family members and that less new information comes through those relationships than comes through our extended relationships with people in many different walks of life. These bridging networks are outward looking and are better for linkages to external assets and for the spreading of information.

A CLOSER LOOK AT COMPLEXITY AND NETWORKS

Those who study complex systems soon get into the tangent study of networks. When you look at a complex system in its intricate detail, you notice that every individual is connected in some way to other individuals. Some connections are stronger, closer, or more numerous for some individuals, and some are weaker or more distant with other individuals, but for every complex system, these networks exist. Thus, complex systems consist of large networks of individuals, all individuals following their own motives and their own sets of rules governing their environments, but a network that has no real central control or leader. These networks might be those formal or informal networks we all have among our families, friends, coworkers, church groups, clubs, and friends of friends. Because of the various conscious and subconscious behaviors in the members of the networks, the behavior of the network is complex and hard to predict. The system produces information and opinions that are transmitted to others in the network—information and opinions that in turn affect other members of the network. Through this behavior that is affected by information and opinions of others, the system adapts, changing behaviors that help the system to survive or succeed; this is a learning process that helps the group evolve over time.

Networks are made up of a combination of focus points, called nodes, connected to other nodes by links. In our context, nodes are primarily people, although companies are often considered nodes as well. Intuitively, we know that some people have more links to others than other people do, and so it is with complex systems. We also know that some people receive more information and communications than others do. These people are considered receiving nodes. Other people send out more communications than they receive and are thus transmitting nodes. Some links are strong and are used often, while other links are more casual and may be used infrequently. Likewise, many of us have close friends as well as a number of people we know who are not part of our close circle of friends. We also have friends of friends, people we have met along the way but have had no real contact with since. All of these networks among a population make for many complex local, regional, national, and international systems.

In a way similar to how Putnam saw the importance of looser ties across extended friendships being more important than close family ties in passing along information, Albert-Laszlo Barabasi, who is an expert on the theories of networks, examined the anonymous mobile phone logs of 20% of Europe over four months. He found that if he removed the people from the network who have many links within their community, the remaining social networks did not fail. If, however, he removed the people with links outside their community, the network suddenly disintegrated. In other words, people with lots of close friends are less important to the stability of network structures than are people with ties to more distant people. What Barabasi drew from this finding was that there is a premium on diversity with a group and in society at large.

In addition, networks change, growing and shrinking as we move, change jobs, marry, divorce, meet new people, get sick, get well, or die, and they have changed over time as culture and "the times" change. Putnam details how since about 1960, Americans have become less connected, doing fewer things together such as neighboring, voting, joining clubs, going to church, and most other things we used to do with others. The phenomenon cuts across all ethnic, racial, age, and income categories. What this may mean is more nodes, meaning individuals, in our networks as time passes, with many weaker links to others and perhaps fewer strong links. This may have an effect on the complexity of the system and how information spreads: who transmits, who receives, how accurately information is passed on (recall the telephone game?), how quickly information is passed on, and the demographics of who receives and transmits and thus the usefulness or importance of the information. Generally speaking, the more nodes there are in a system, the more complex it is, which in turn means that the transmission and receipt of information is changed, slower in some places and faster in others, more reliable in one place than another, or not passed on at all in parts of the network. Also, over time, our networks adapt to our needs. Sometimes we need medical help we've never needed before and the people who provide help get added to our network. If one of our friends moves, our network evolves. Our child meets new friends at school and brings other families into our world.

When my family first moved to Indianapolis, my wife needed to find a hairdresser, so I asked my new secretary at work, who happened to lived not far from our new home, whom she might recommend. My wife went to the recommended hairdresser and quickly met people who changed much of our lives. We eventually bought the farmhouse the hairdresser lived in, which brought new friends and adventures to our children, and in their opinion, it became our best home ever. Those new friendships were also the start of the path that led me eventually into my prefession as a college professor. I wouldn't be writing this book if my wife had not gone to that hairdresser. Given such connections, you can see how predicting economic, political, or any other type of behavior is difficult if accuracy is required. We know that in some cases, we can see trends or general directions, such as weather forecasts, but the further into the future we try to predict, the worse the accuracy.

Can we measure how complex a system is? Intuitively, we think the answer must be yes. Just by observation, we can see that some networks and systems are more complex than others. When I was in the US Air Force, my job was in cryptography—codes used to transmit classified information over long distances. It was—and still is—done by computers and various forms of electronic transmission methods. We used to use computers that generated random electronic signals. There were different levels of randomness that we controlled. In many ways, the types of computers and signals we generated created complex systems that computers receiving the messages could make sense of and decode a message. The system adapted and changed in a specific way. We could control how complex the signal was, but we didn't mathematically come up with a measure of its complexity. The same problem exists in the study of complex systems. Because the study of complex systems is still relatively new, a single theory does not yet exist to describe complex systems, and thus the terms describing central concepts have not yet been adequately defined—terms like *information, computation,* and *order*. Until we can agree on definitions, we can't really come up with a specific measure of concepts. Math is very precise and needs specific definitions to be useful.

Because complex systems and networks change and adapt, they are called dynamic. Because they change, especially as we look at economics, we desire to predict their behavior, to tell people what's going to happen in the future as the system goes through its changes. We used to believe that with enough information, we could predict anything, even for all time, an idea espoused by a mathematician named Pierre Simon Laplace in the early 1800s. Then in 1927, along came Werner Heisenberg, who gave us the "uncertainty principle." The uncertainty principle was first applied to the physics of quantum mechanics—the study of subatomic particles. It basically says that you can either predict the position of a particle or its momentum, but not both. You can tell where the particle is but not how it is moving, or you can say how it is moving but not where it is. The real heart of the idea is that just by observing the particle, you change something about its position and motion; you can never be certain of the information about the particle just because you try to look at it. Of course, this made Laplace's idea of predicting everything for all time if you had enough information a nice idea but impossible because we will never have enough information just because we try to find it. Most people, however, said that the uncertainty principle applied only to quantum mechanics and was thus a special case and that we should be able to predict things in the non-quantum world. It was chaos, however, that finally ended the idea of Laplace.

CHAOS

The term *chaos* is probably a misnomer. Chaos is the study of specific kinds of systems that have certain characteristics. While chaotic systems are also complex systems, one of the uses of chaos theories is allowing us to examine how systems change over time. The characteristic we are interested in here is that very small differences in the conditions at a beginning point of a change will evolve into huge differences in the system over time. For example, weather predictions are fairly accurate for a period of a few days to perhaps a week, but beyond that, they are not of much use if you want to plan a picnic. Very small conditions in today's weather in another part of the country will affect the direction or severity of a storm system by the time it arrives in your location. A similar effect is seen in economics. If we want to predict economic conditions in the future, it is impossible to know all the smallest details of the economy today at the starting point that will cause change and be part of the system that evolves into the economic conditions of some point in the future. We might be able to give an approximation, but only with some level of uncertainty.

The reason this happens is found in the concept of *nonlinearity*. In a linear relationship, the result of change is simply the sum of the parts of the thing that changes. For example, earlier, we briefly introduced the equation $Y = C + I + G + NX$ as representing the way to determine the gross domestic product, GDP. Here, GDP is the sum of the parts of the economy, namely consumption, investment, government spending, and net exports. Thus, it is a linear equation, meaning that there is a direct relationship between GDP and the sum of the four parts of the economy. A nonlinear system is different. In a nonlinear system, the whole is different than the sum of its parts. In a linear system, the parts of the system don't interact to create anything new, but in a nonlinear system, the parts of the system do interact and create something new. The end product is not just the sum of the system's parts but is different in unexpected ways because we don't know what all the parts are to start with.

To explain this concept, Melanie Mitchell gives an example of breeding rabbits on an island. If each pair of rabbits has four offspring a year and then dies, the system is linear and the number of rabbits is known at any given time. The system becomes nonlinear if we introduce more reality into the system. If one of the four offspring dies before it breeds, the resulting number of rabbits on the island changes. If the island becomes overcrowded and food and space become limited, the effect on breeding will change. A storm could wipe out a portion of the population. The resulting population changes in ways we could not predict at the beginning because we didn't know that a storm would develop from faraway weather patterns or that some of the offspring would unexpectedly die.

Likewise, because we can never have enough knowledge about all the parts that will affect an economy for good or ill, we will find it impossible to know how that economy will look at any given point in the future. This is especially true if part of the system is not based on market forces but rather is political and results from the decisions of a group of people who, by definition, will almost certainly make few rational, logical decisions even if they had all the information. Thus, the system looks as though it is chaotic—hence the name—and we just can't know what will happen next. If we could somehow have enough knowledge about all the things that would affect the system, it wouldn't look chaotic and we could understand it and make predictions. We don't have that knowledge, however, so the system appears to be chaotic. Because such systems only *appear* to be chaotic, it means that some of the effects we see in a complex system can also be seen in chaotic systems and thus appear unpredictable in large part. Let's examine the phenomenon of synchrony as an example.

SYNCHRONY

Steven Strogatz, in his book *Sync: How Order Emerges from Chaos in the Universe, Nature, and Daily Life,* writes, "Scientists have long been baffled by the existence of spontaneous order in the universe. The laws of thermodynamics seem to dictate the opposite." The laws of thermodynamics basically say that things go from order to disorder, meaning they decay or rust away, for example. When we find order coming out of disorder, that deserves a closer look. Strogatz goes on to say that finding such spontaneous order in *time,* such that the same things happen at the same time, is remarkably subtle. This type of order is called synchrony.

Strogatz tells of large groups of fireflies that begin flashing their lights together after initially flashing in an apparently random fashion. Similar events happen with crickets chirping, frogs croaking, gaps in the asteroid belt, alpha waves in the brain, and the electricity cycles of alternating current generated in power plants, to name just a few. Synchronized behavior evolving out of chaotic behavior is all around us. Many phenomena exhibit waves of highs and lows in activity, even in human behavior. The study of these synchronous behaviors is a relatively new science, but one that is opening new understandings not only of physical events but also of the behavior we see in the animal and human worlds.

How can different insects, power plants, or people synchronize their behavior, even some behaviors they do not consciously control? (For example, the menstrual cycles of women living together will often synchronize.) We can look at individual insects, people, or power plants, for example, as the nodes of a network that are linked to other nodes in the network in various ways. They can have strong or weak links; some can be transmitters while others are receivers; some are nearby and others are at a distance. Inside the network, however, one of the apparent prerequisites for synchrony is proximity of the individuals in the group—they are connected in some way and thus can transmit information or influence to others.

Let's look at an example used by Strogatz to demonstrate how synchronization works. Imagine a toilet with a tank that is filling with water from some external source. The tank is rigged so that when the water reaches a certain level, the toilet flushes again. In essence, it's perpetually filling and flushing in an endless cycle.

Now imagine that the toilet is part of a system of similar toilets, all flushing when the water in their tanks reaches a certain level, and all tied together by pipes so that when they flush, the water that leaves their tanks flows to the other toilets, adding to the water in those tanks. At the beginning of our example, the toilets are all flushing at randomly different times. This means that when our original toilet flushes, it brings each of the other toilets closer to the point of flushing. Some will flush soon after one other toilet flushes, whereas others will come near to the required water level but still not close enough to flush. Others will already be flushing when water comes in from other toilets and thus will fill faster once that part of their cycle begins again. Over time, the toilets will begin flushing at the same time as each is pushed to the critical water level faster and faster. The toilets can only flush so fast, however, and soon, the toilets will all be pushed to their limits by being filled by other toilets so quickly. If you think about it a little, you may also see that the cycles will begin to match in toilets nearest each other first because the distance the water has to flow in the pipes is shorter and the tanks will fill to the critical limits together in a shorter time than in toilets separated by greater distance. Which groups of toilets start syncing soon will vary, depending on where they were in their cycles at the beginning of the experiment. Some will take longer to sync at the beginning of the experiment than those that are near each other. Thus, although the whole system will eventually come into sync, with all toilets flushing at the same time, the pattern of how that happens will be different each time the experiment is run. This is because of the differences in the conditions of the nodes, the toilets, at the beginning, which is what makes it difficult to make predictions in a chaotic system.

This kind of process is seen in the cycles in nature, the universe, and human behavior. The process of fireflies synchronizing their flashing looks very similar, with individuals located close together starting to flash in sync and the size of those groups spreading until they merge with the synchronized flashing of other groups so that eventually, the entire system is going through its on-off cycle at the same time. In fact, similar patterns are seen wherever synchrony occurs, where groups of individuals get cycle-type inputs from others in the group and begin to sync. So the question becomes, do humans exhibit this same behavior?

James Crutchfield of the Complexity Science Center at the University of California at Davis wrote *The Hidden Fragility of Complex Systems—Consequences of Change, Changing Consequences,* in which he describes how, over time, complex systems become increasingly complex. In fact, he says, they also become multidimensional, with layers of new functions and additional complexity changing the previous functions of the system. Then, he adds, things change when you add intelligence to the system, because intelligence allows increased memory and sophisticated strategies. The result is that by anticipating each other's moves, "agents" in the system start chasing or anticipating each other's changing strategies. Soon, the group behavior starts to oscillate. This takes the place of unintelligent agents that would or could not adapt to the changes in the system. In other words, adding intelligence to the system allows for adaptation, memory of past behaviors and the outcomes that resulted, and repetition of successful behaviors and elimination of unsuccessful behaviors. This begins a synchrony as patterns are repeated by several agents over time. People make the difference.

If we think about people living in close proximity to others, we intuitively know that each person has a different level of information and motivations regarding any given topic than the others. We also know that the people have links of various strengths and lengths with others in the group and thus receive and send information to others in the group, which is in turn received and perceived through various motivations and personalities. Some of the received information is assimilated, some is passed on through networks, some is rejected, some is stored for later retrieval, and some is forgotten. Some people will have outlooks and opinions similar to those of others in their group, while others will have different outlooks and opinions.

You can see how a complex system is present and that when information is received from outside the group and passed on through the network of the one receiving the information first, the information is likely to be passed to others who have closer links to that originator and who are thus more likely to have similar opinions or outlooks. The second person who receives the information then passes it along to his or her network, and the information spreads like the water in the toilet system described above. Because some people have more network connections than others, they will likely receive the information earlier and pass it along to more people, thus becoming focal points of subgroups in the system. These subgroups of closely aligned members start syncing first, and as their networks assimilate the information at different times and in different strengths, and because of the strengths and lengths of their links with others, the whole system receives the information in a manner that looks chaotic. The synchrony spreads from the subgroups until a large part of the whole network is in sync. Not everyone will be in sync, but enough will be synchronized to drive an overall opinion or behavior for the group. If we were to try to represent the opinion or action of the group with a numerical measure, that number would be an average that represents the position of the group over some time period. This is because at any point in time, the group will have a range of opinions, but over time, we can see the overall average opinion or action of the group.

Sociologist Mark Granovetter did work on how fads spread. He demonstrated the effect by using the example of a mob of 100 people and their decision to riot or not. In his example, a person decides to riot or not based on the decisions of others around him. Those who are instigators will begin to riot even if no one else is rioting. Others need to see some critical mass of others rioting before they will join in. That critical number of others taking action is spread across the crowd in a probability distribution. Granovetter then assumed that each person had his own threshold of motivation before he would join the riot, and he assigned a numerical value to that threshold so that everyone in the crowd had a threshold between 0 and 99, representing the number of other people they need to see involved in rioting before they will join. The person with a 0 is ready to start rioting even if no one else is. A person with a threshold of 1 joins in quickly, seeing one other person begin to riot. Now, with two people rioting, a person with a threshold of 2 joins in and the rioting grows as more people reach their critical thresholds, until everyone is rioting. Next, Granovetter changed the composition of the group by changing the threshold of the person with a 1 to a threshold of 2. Then when the instigator, the 0 threshold person, begins to riot, no one in the group joins in because there is no one who will join in with only one other person making trouble, and thus, no riot develops. Granovetter showed that even though the makeup of the second group is nearly identical and has been changed only the slightest amount, the outcome is very different from that of the first group. One of the critical assumptions in Granovetter's example is that everyone has the same level of knowledge as everyone else, something that is rarely true in reality.

Like the popularity of books, movies, and music, most fads are a result of herd behavior in which most people rely on the behavior of others to guide their own behavior. Now imagine that everyone in a network is subjected to these kinds of stimuli and has to make a choice: buy the new technology or not, dress like others in the group or not, join the latest dance craze or not, or vote for the same candidates for the same reasons or not. It is easy to see how groupthink can take hold quickly and how groups of people can get in sync. Synchronizing may not all start at the same time, because it takes some time for the information-decision-behavior cycle to spread. Even so, they cycle does spread, and a level of synchrony does occur—maybe not perfect synchrony, but certainly recognizable synchronized behavior.

Werner Heisenberg, the author of the uncertainty principle, once observed, "When one wishes to calculate the 'the future' from 'the present' one can only get statistical results since one can never discover every detail of the present." That is the case in complex systems such as economies.

A related question must be asked at this point. When we speak of cyclical activities such as individuals in a complex or chaotic system coming into sync, we have so far assumed that the activities are of the same kind, such as flushing toilets, herd mentality, flashing fireflies, and so forth. What about different but related types of activities that are part of the same system? Will those activities come into sync with other related but different activities in the system? For example, in the expansion part of an economic cycle, we tend to see increases in consumption as people make more purchases. Is there also a change in other components of GDP that are related to consumption, so that there is some level of synchronization between consumption, investment, government spending, and net exports? The answer to the question is yes, as will be discussed a little later.

CITIES

The kinds of networks and groups we've been discussing exist everywhere, and the links between people can span great distances; however, there is a reason why cities are more effective and efficient than rural areas in creating new ideas, making money, and providing better education, health care, and longer life expectancies: They have more people. With a concentration of people and their networks, cities can provide much more of just about everything than can small towns or rural areas. We all know cities that are good places to live as well as cities that aren't. Each city has its own personality, its own strengths and its own weaknesses, and the world is becoming more urban every day. In 2012, cities became the dwelling place for more than half the world's population, a trend that shows no sign of slowing.

Cities are full of complex systems of all kinds: networks not only of people but also of businesses, governments, and the mechanical and electrical connections we have made. Some are more "networked" than others in that they are hubs of communications networks that have more links to other networks and nodes than other cities do. Think of New York City and Los Angeles, which have more extensive centers of communication than smaller cities such as Houston or Miami. New York and Los Angeles are often seen as places that are trendsetters while the cities in the Midwest lag in accepting new trends. The cultures of some cities are more accepting of new ideas, or even the attempts to develop new ideas, than other cities are. Silicon Valley is such an area, especially compared to smaller rural areas that resist change or new ideas. It has been said that in the Palo Alto, California, area near the Silicon Valley industrial area, if you hadn't failed four times in trying to start a new company, you hadn't succeeded. The effects on the strength of network links, as well as on the types of information on the networks in those areas, would be significant compared with places that frowned on failure. Edward Glaeser, in his book *Triumph of the City,* notes that "to survive, cities must attract smart people and enable them to work collaboratively....The best cities have a mix of skills and provide pathways for those who start with less and end with more." There has been much written on what makes cities work or fail; most of the success or failure has to do with programs, physical infrastructure, and cultures that facilitate people interacting with each other.

Cities are the major players in economic activity not only because most people live in urban settings but also because cities generate most of the innovations that turn into the new or improved products we buy. We have seen a trend develop over recent decades in which the most referenced scientific papers are written by multiple authors. Many fewer lone geniuses are developing new ideas than in the past. Collaboration is becoming the norm, especially because these collaborations are possible with Internet communication allowing not only quick written and verbal communication but also the exchange of huge amounts of data and photographic and graphic information. These collaborations, either local or at a distance, allow researchers and theorists to test and refine ideas with the input of other experts. The Internet allows for access to laboratories, libraries, and field researchers that used to take much longer. The number of nodes and links in the networks has expanded dramatically, and the vast majority of this expansion has occurred in cities around the world.

The problem with this interconnectivity, Steven Strogatz says, is that failures in the system can also spread quickly and far in all directions. An electric grid, for example, has protective devices that can choke off entire cities when an unexpected power surge happens. Sudden drops in consumption can cause concerns in some instances, as well. Where can such changes in electric demand on such a scale come from? They happen, but in a complex system, where and when they will occur is nearly impossible to predict. When the O. J. Simpson verdict was read, the entire power grid experienced a drop in consumption as millions of people turned off their television sets simultaneously.

Complex systems are heavily interconnected throughout our world economies. These interconnected systems include utilities, computerized payment systems, foreign exchange markets, and book lending at local library branches. Buying a hat at Walmart sets off a signal to suppliers and manufacturers in a complex Internet system as payment is made at the checkout counter. Signals are sent in all directions for keeping track of inventory, taking money from your bank account and sending it to pay the supplier in China for the hat, ordering a new hat to put on the shelf to replace the one you bought, and paying the employee who swiped your card at the checkout counter. Multiply that by all the transactions made by all the retailers in the world, and you can see that many things can cause surprises in such systems.

To take our examination of interconnectivity a little further, let's look briefly at the European Union. There are currently 27 members of the union, 17 of which use the euro as currency. The European Union is a group of separate countries with various economic conditions and political systems so that problems in some countries spread quickly to others. Johan Van Overtveldt, in *The End of the Euro*, lists eight factors from the theories of the "optimum currency area" that are needed for a smoothly functioning monetary union: (1) the mobility of factors of production, especially labor; (2) price and wage flexibility; (3) similar inflation rates; (4) the degree of openness of the individual economies; (5) the degree of diversification of the individual economies; (6) financial integration; (7) fiscal integration; (8) political integration. In other words, these separate countries have to be similar to the states in the United States where each state has its own government, but there is a federal government that governs the nation as a whole. If these eight factors are present, he wrote, "fulfillment of these eight factors will synchronize the business cycle throughout the monetary union. If the cycle is well synchronized, the need for nation-specific macroeconomic policies will be reduced."

The EU countries had to take on these characteristics so that the details of what made Europe, well, Europe could not be hidden beneath the old ways they tended to use to make themselves appear better than they were. The way complex systems work, exposing the truth of how individual pieces of sand affect all the other pieces of sand in the pile, means that we have to look at economies in a different way than using the standard numbers and theories that have provided overall insights but have not allowed us to really know what's going on and what's likely to happen next, making the sand pile look stable when in reality it is on the edge of collapse and it takes only another grain of sand to change everything. As noted by Mr. Dryden in the movie *Lawrence of Arabia,* big things have small beginnings.

Like the grains of sand in the sand pile, all cities are different from others. We easily recognize that some cities prosper and some do not. As it works out, those cities that are centers of innovation are also more prosperous than those with little innovation happening in them. What is also significant for urban prosperity is how well cities are networked with other cities. As Richard Florida has shown in his writings on cities and creativity, cities that have more jobs that require innovation are more connected to other cities that have higher concentrations of innovation. Less prosperous cities have fewer networks with innovation. Florida notes in *Who's Your City* that "population density is a rudimentary measure of economic activity that does not fully convey the vast gulf separating the world's most productive regions from the rest" (p. 20). The two largest regions for economic growth are the greater Tokyo region, which produces $2.5 trillion in economic output annually, and the region stretching from Boston through New York City and to Washington, DC, which produces about $2.2 trillion. The region from Chicago to Pittsburgh comes in third at $1.6 trillion. Although population levels and economic activity are usually correlated, the real difference in economic activity correlates with the level of innovation, which is even more concentrated into certain areas. It is innovation, as you recall, that changes and adapts to the complex economic system. Regions with high economic activity have concentrations of universities, flexible labor markets, high-powered companies, and venture capital to help turn new ideas into businesses. There aren't many places with this combination of resources. The places with this combination of resources create nodes and are well connected to innovation networks that drive changes in technology and ideas in the rest of the system, in the same way information, ideas, trends, and fads are spread.

Jonah Lehrer, in *Imagine: How Creativity Works,* says that all new ideas come from the same place:

> "There is a network of neurons in the brain, and then the network shifts. All of a sudden, electricity flows in an unfamiliar pattern, a shiver of current across a circuit board of cells. Even so, sometimes a single network is not enough. Sometimes a creative problem is so difficult that it requires people to connect their imaginations together; the answer only arrives if we collaborate. That's because a group is more than just a collection of individual talents. Instead it is a chance for those talents to exceed themselves, to produce something greater than anyone thought possible." (p. 139)

That's the magic of cities: There is a much greater chance the right mix of people will find each other, and more neurons will connect in new ways than was possible before.

Lynne Zucker and Michael Darby in their research have found these concentrations in certain regions of the United States in Boston, New York City, and Washington-Baltimore on the East Coast; San Francisco, Seattle, and Los Angeles in the West; and Chicago in the Midwest. As these places tend to illustrate, scientific advances and commercial innovation can be highly concentrated into relatively few nodes in the economic networks.

Richard Florida has found something similar but takes it a step further. He has found that cities and regions have sorted themselves into different class lines. Different classes of people have long sorted themselves into neighborhoods. Now, however, we find a re-sorting of people into cities and regions on a nationwide scale. Some regions are becoming centers of what Florida calls the "creative class," whereas other regions are made up of larger shares of working-class or service-class people. Florida points out that the centers of the creative class are becoming the clear economic winners. The large working-class centers are generally more stagnant. Some service-class centers, such as Las Vegas, are growing and attracting jobs, but the jobs tend to be pay low wages and have little chance for advancement. Even though larger cities have their advantages for creativity and economic success, they do not have the corner on the market of creative jobs. Many smaller cities are doing well. They tend to be college towns and a few other regions in Illinois, Florida, Alabama, New Mexico, and Idaho. The nucleus of the creative class, however, is rather concentrated in Raleigh-Durham; San Francisco; Washington, DC; and Rochester, NY, with Boston; Seattle; and Hartford, Connecticut, close behind.

As the needs for new technology and innovation become more important and their use becomes more and more prevalent in the economy, success for companies, and therefore investors in those companies, increasingly depend on the economic and public policy environment that allows companies to succeed, so if we are to see how our economy will do, we will have to see if our cities provide the environment for success.

Such an environment must include adequate communications infrastructure, meaningful incentives, excellent education systems, helpful and stable government policies, and a concentration of technical skills and experience. Generally, these things exist where there is a culture that embraces new ideas.

There is a story told by Joshua Ramo about Michael Moritz, a legendary Silicon Valley venture capitalist who picked several huge winners out of crowded fields of new ideas and startup companies. Moritz's way of looking at the field and picking the stars was based on thinking differently than others, looking for and seeing things that others didn't. Moritz was educated in literature, and although he appreciated technology, he was not particularly technologically competent, especially compared to those who came looking for money. For Moritz, the technology of a company was not the point; the point was the context, the environment the company was headed into and how the company would be able to change and adapt quickly, leading the change rather than responding to the environment. Could the people in the company read what was going on around them, anticipate what the market needed and how it was changing, and adapt before the market went that direction and, in making the change, perhaps change the direction the market was going? In other words, Moritz didn't look at the sand pile that appeared to be stable; he looked at the grains of sand inside the pile and saw how unstable the pile really was. The process he used requires a combination of deduction, insight, and inference. Advance signs of change are likely to appear when we look in unexpected places. In fact, in a world that is as connected as ours, the advance signs of change appear *first* when we look in unexpected places.

In a similar way, we can look at the economic sand pile in the complex system of networks in cities, skills, infrastructure, local government programs, and local education systems; we can look at those grains of sand for which we already collect information and see how they are behaving and changing and can perhaps come much closer to a true description of the business cycle and of larger changes in the economy.

In *The Atlas of the Hinterworld*, created by the geography department of Loughborough University in England, is a description of the interconnectivity of many cities with other cities of the world. The study includes 123 cities, including several in the United States. As would be expected, all of the cities had varying levels of connection with other cities, mostly based on transportation connection. Thus, Indianapolis had strong connections with Minneapolis and weak connections with Sofia, Bulgaria; however, it had *some* connections with Sofia, which indicates how diverse the sand pile is. Looking at the economic regional areas across the United States produced by the Bureau of Economic Analysis, we see economic connections. We can do this by examining the similarities and performances of those economies. For example, generally, high-growth states are close to other high-growth states. Likewise, low-growth states are near other low-growth states. Between the two groups are moderate-growth areas.

If we look at the world's 100 largest economies, we see that 37 belong to metropolitan areas in the United States. In fact, total gross product of our metro economies ($13 trillion) is equal to 24% of the production of the 200 largest countries (excluding the United States) and is greater than the combined production of 178 of those countries. Clearly, our metropolitan areas not only play a major role domestically but are also critical to the world economy, partly through the connectivity they have.

Y = C + I + G + NX REVISITED

If we are going to understand the movements of each component of Y = C + I + G + NX, we need to understand how they are moved by the actions of people in complex systems. In the United States, consumption makes up about 70% of GDP, and consumption is also the most integrated of the complex systems in the formula; each consumer is a node in the network of the system and thus, there are hundreds of millions of nodes. This means that there will likely be a stronger reaction in GDP when consumption increases or decreases. Not all consumers buy every product, so even the category of consumption has several networks within it. Some groups of consumers buy a wide variety of similar products. Other groups of consumers buy few products or buy very specialized products that few others will purchase. We also know that several forces cause people to change their purchases of goods and services. These forces are not felt uniformly across all consumers and are not felt simultaneously. Over time, people react differently and with differing intensities to trends, fads, special promotions, inducements, advertisements, and needs. Because these trends and inducements are often publicized widely, we can often see how they can spark behavior of several consumers at the same time and thus spark the beginnings of synchrony. This synchronized behavior, if sufficient, eventually causes movement of consumption from several sources moving together in a similar direction. Spending on clothing might move relative to spending on other goods and services at the same time. Spending on technology items such as home computers may not be directly related to spending on clothing. They are different markets, but they both tend to follow changes in disposable income, which might be looked at as the water from an outside source that is filling the toilet tank.

Because having disposable income is related to employment, which in turn is related to business investments, it is easy to see that the investment component of GDP will move in the same direction at a similar time, with perhaps a lag, as companies invest in new factories and equipment in response to increased consumption. The lag will be short if unused manufacturing capacity is brought back online. Some increases in employment will be the result of the increased investment in the factory and/or equipment, and some will come later, when workers are hired as the factory makes its products. Investment and employment are also related to net exports as the products made in the United States are sent to markets overseas, and thus we can see how each component of GDP might join in the synchrony. Therefore, consumption, investment, government spending, and net export each add to the strength and timing of the cycles of GDP. The contribution of each component to the total movement of GDP depends on how well each component syncs with the other components; the greater the sync between the components, the greater the effect on GDP. The start of the process may see the components at different levels and in different cycles, like the network of toilets, but over time, the synchrony will become stronger, creating the expansionary phase of a business cycle.

Government spending is different than consumption, investment, and net exports. It is the only component of GDP that is not directly related to market forces. It is based on political decisions. Thus, it may or may not increase or decrease in sync with the market forces driving the other components. In fact, it may be counter-cyclical or move counter to the movement of the other components as government attempts to stimulate a declining economy or to slow an economy that is expanding too fast. The movement of government spending will thus not normally be in sync with the other components and therefore either reduces or enhances the effect the other components have on GDP. If it moves counter to the other components, it will dampen those components' overall effect on GDP. If it moves in the same direction, it will enhance the effect of the other components. This effect can determine the level of success of the outcome of the government's intended policy.

We will look at the topic of *big data* a little later. For now, simply know that it takes advantage of our ability to generate enormous amounts of data that often reveals correlations and relationships that may help our ability to predict many events. Big data might also identify relationships we may not have known existed before. The key to understanding big data is that at its heart is finding correlations that show what the relationships between phenomena are but not to show why the relationships exist. Cause and effect are difficult to determine mathematically in any event, and big data does not go down that path. In the next chapter, we will look at it briefly and discuss its implications. Right now, let's look at some correlations.

If we can show various correlations between consumption, investment, government spending, and net exports with changes in GDP, as complex as those relationships are, we can show which ones affect GDP the most and then perhaps what causes business cycles. As it turns out, there have been several correlation analyses of these relationships (for example, one by Robert Hodrick and Edward Prescott in 2009, and another by Martin Eichenbaum and Kenneth Singleton in 1986) that show that such correlations exist.

Not surprisingly, the strongest correlations of GDP changes are with the consumption of services and nondurable goods as well as with nonresidential investments and investments in machinery. All of these tend to be short-term spending by consumers and businesses. When we look at the timing of changes in GDP and the various components, the first changes that occur ahead of changes in GDP are those relating to production, specifically the workweek and hours worked, both of which are related to income. At about the same time, we see a decline in consumption, which would be expected with fears of lower future income. Soon after those changes, we see a slowing in the velocity of money as people spend less money, and the speed with which a dollar flows through the economy slows down as consumption falls. This is quickly followed by reduction in fixed investments (spending on factory machines) and reduction in inventories. Then we watch the money supply fall, and finally, investment in durable investments (long-term assets like factories) drops. Interestingly, changes in GDP itself do not happen until just before changes in the money supply. In fact, we don't see the reaction of the Federal Reserve (the Fed) until after major changes have already occurred. Government response tends to be a lagging indicator. If we look at the whole series of changes from the first to the last, we also see that the first changes are short term in nature (workweek/hours, consumption of nondurables and services) and the later changes are in long-term components (durable capital spending). We can thus follow the changes through the economy, but the changes start with a reduction in the hours people work and in employment. Let's look at how that happens and also why.

The first event seems to be a shortening of the workweek. Often, this relates to the fact that the economies at its peak and may be inching past the full employment level of output where inflation is likely and productivity, and thus profits, begins to fall as inventories start to rise. Beyond this full employment level, we can see overtime increasing, and this reduction in the workweek may relate to a reduction in overtime as employers try to get back to the higher productivity that occurs at their most efficient level of production. At first, this usually means cutting overtime hours. As the incomes of those workers decline, so do their purchases, primarily of nondurable items. As consumption falls, producers start cutting back on making some of those nondurable products, and eventually, that means cutting back on the regular hours of the workforce and perhaps cutting the number of workers. As the decline begins, it is not difficult to follow the progression down the list of events that lead to the decline in GDP. This progression is a description of what Keynes wrote about when he said that the marginal productivity of capital starts to decline. That's what happens when we start working overtime and the machines have to work longer and perhaps faster than at their most efficient level.

There can be other reasons for consumption to decline, however—shocks that we mentioned earlier. Shocks to economic systems come in many forms. They are often unexpected, although some are predicted or maybe predictable. They are events that interfere with normal economic activity: natural disasters, such as hurricanes, and wars and terrorist attacks, such as 9/11. They could also be political: changes in import quotas or tariffs, changes in currency values that interrupt trade between countries, strikes that stop the flow of supplies or delivery of products, or a breakdown of international financial markets. The shocks aren't always negative; they could be higher than expected improvements in productivity or the environment. There are thus many ways to affect economic activity that may or may not involve government taxation and spending but still are not caused initially by market activities. When they do occur, economic or non-economic forces can cause an economic downturn and test how resilient economies are politically, financially, and socially. They tell us how government and the markets respond to surprises that occur in the sand pile. Resilience is the key to the strength of an economy in the long run, more than consumption, investment, government spending, net exports, employment, GDP, or anything else. If the economy can handle surprises without major losses of jobs and the value of what is owned, it is a good economy. That's why we need knowledge of the small details of how our economy works—so we can make decisions on issues that allow us to adjust and adapt to the big surprises that affect everyone.

Nate Silver, in *The Signal and the Noise,* points out that each year, the government produces data on 45,000 economic indicators and that private providers of information produce as many as four million statistics. Selecting the right information from among such a huge database to make a prediction, or even to determine the current state of affairs, is as unlikely as finding meaningful results from analyzing the data. In addition, to make a prediction about the direction of a business cycle, we have to have a beginning point from which the prediction is made. The data themselves, however, are constantly being revised over periods of months and sometimes years. During that time, the economy is also changing, so that behavior of the economy in one business cycle may not be repeated in subsequent cycles. Then consider that even if you could get good, current information, it is most likely affected by past policy decisions to stimulate or slow the economy, so you would end up analyzing data that had been influenced or was being influenced by past policy, perhaps to add additional policy. It's like adding another medicine on top of what you're already taking. How will they interact and what will the results be?

If the movements of GDP define whether we are in an expansion or recession, then the detailed reasons for the movement must also be more clearly defined. Traditionally, there have been several explanations for the existence of business cycles. Several of these explanations say that there is no real reason why business cycles exist. (We'll go through the theories about business cycles in the next section.)

The point here is that business cycles exist and the theories that attempt to explain them must make certain assumptions in order to work. These theories have been very useful, and I do not intend to make light of the contributions they have made to our understanding. The assumptions about human behavior that they must make in order to work are not found in the real world, however. For example, to study the effect of changing prices on the level of demand for a product, a number of assumptions are made to allow us to study just the change in prices and to eliminate other factors that also affect the levels of demand. Thus, we make the assumption that people make rational decisions when they purchase goods or services. Coupled with this assumption is the assumption that every consumer has all the information that other consumers in the market have. Making these assumptions allows people to analyze the information and decide whether or not to make their purchases. We also assume that no consumer or seller can affect the price of the product so that the price is not artificially changed by the participants in the market for their own purposes. We then assume that there is perfect competition in the market so that people are free to enter or leave the market at any time and do not have to buy or sell the good or service because of some compunction but are doing so voluntarily.

As you can see, these assumptions allow us to study how prices are determined in such circumstances, and how they might change and affect the supply and demand of a good or service. Such markets, however, do not exist; no one has the information other buyers of products have; no one makes buying and selling decisions rationally. Even if they want to make decisions rationally, they don't have the information needed, and the information basically comes from the seller and is almost always incomplete. The seller establishes the prices with price tags and perhaps with a superior bargaining position because of his or her superior product knowledge (think of buying a car). Thus, consumers really don't know what a good or fair price for the product is. In this way, supply and demand are not independent of each other in the real world. Suppliers affect the factors that are supposed to determine the market price, rather than the price being determined by the interaction of buyers and sellers. The buyers have significantly less input. There are always reasons to buy or sell, and many of them involve buyers and sellers having a true need or a desire based on the psychological need: the desire to fit in; the desire to look wise or smart; being required to do so for a job, a friend, or family; doing so for entertainment, and so on. Entering and leaving the market is thus not as easy as the assumptions imply.

What complex systems allow us to do is take the next steps beyond what we learn from theories and to move to descriptions of the economy that more closely resemble real-world conditions. Next, we will look at the aggregate economy, where we examine how the complex-system approach can help us understand the big picture.

CHAPTER 5

KEYNES AND MESSY BUSINESS CYCLES

> In the classic old business cycle, there would be a diminution in sales; it would take a little while for this information to reach corporate headquarters. And there would be an inventory pileup. And then—bam—business would react, sometimes violently, by cutting production.
>
> —Alan Blinder

To get a better understanding about how business cycles work and what causes them, we need to know something about what business cycles are and how our current approaches to defining and affecting them developed. Hopefully, from our earlier discussions, you will have a feeling for why, when we add complexity into the mix, our predictions have over the long run been about as good as guessing.

John Maynard Keynes, in *The General Theory of Employment, Interest and Money,* said that the business cycle exists because of this relationship between the marginal propensity to consume and the marginal efficiency of capital. As long as capital (the combination of manufacturing and technology) was sufficient to supply the things we wanted to buy, the prices would remain stable. But there was a need to have a return on the investments in machines and technology, and Keynes said that the required return had to be higher than the prevailing interest rate in the economy. If the return was at or below the prevailing rate of interest, then why would a business go through all the time, expense, and hassle of expanding? If a business did not expand, output would fall, causing the business cycle to go into a recession. If the return was higher than the prevailing interest rate, the company would invest in new machines and technology, and output would increase and the business cycle would move into an expansion.

Although these changes in the marginal propensity to consume and the marginal efficiency in capital can generally explain business cycles, it is difficult to use them to predict the size, duration, and beginning or end of a cycle. Business cycles are, so far, an ongoing feature of the economy. The standard theories tend to explain *changes* in the business cycle by pointing to major innovations or new technologies. Even more often, the theories focus on "shocks" to the system, including supply shocks, policy shocks, natural disasters, and similar events. These shocks do seem to cause some changes in the "normal" frequency or strength of the business cycle from time to time. There are several reasons for the difficulty in using shocks and innovations to make predictions of economic activity. For example, there is always a lag before information about economic activity is available; it takes time for the government to gather and publish economic information. In the rush to get the information out, there are sometimes errors or incomplete information involved so that the data is revised later to be more accurate. It's also very difficult to know where we are in a business cycle relative to the peak or trough. Do new data mean we have reached the peak and will now start down or that we have reached a trough and will start improving? Do the data reflect a pause in growth or recession?

Because we're trying to describe a complex system, we have to understand the effects of rumors, fads, trends, and even ego or biases in interpretations, so let's look more closely at the increases and decreases in the exchanges of money for products in the marketplace, as they define whether the economy is expanding or contracting. Exchanges in the marketplace are basically described in the concepts of supply and demand, the idea that the higher the price people will pay for a product or service, the more of those products the maker will be willing to sell. On the other side of the transaction, the higher the price, the fewer products the people will be willing to buy. The right number of products to make (supply) will be equal to the number of products that people are willing to buy (demand) at a given price. The meeting of that price and that quantity is called the market's equilibrium.

If instead of looking at the production of one product or service, we look at them all, then we are looking at the production of all goods and services, which is the definition of gross domestic product (GDP). When we look at GDP, we are looking for the output of all goods and services that will be produced at various price *levels* in the economy. Equilibrium between price levels and total output is reached when price levels are sufficient for companies to produce goods and services and to make a sufficient profit. In other words, we're looking for stable prices, full employment, and profitable companies over time, which happens at equilibrium. Things, however, change in the complex real world, and equilibrium is fleeting. With changes in innovation and consumption caused by shocks and/or changes in returns on capital, those equilibrium prices go up and down over time and we get business cycles.

Do these fluctuations in market equilibrium prices really tell us how business cycles work and what causes them?

MARKET EQUILIBRIUM?

When we look at the concept of market "equilibrium" prices, we can come to some surprising conclusions. The first is that we can never be sure that the price that prevails for any given product or service really is the equilibrium price. There is no way for any of us to know that at that price, the supply of the product is equal to the demand for it. The second conclusion is that we have an incorrect concept of what equilibrium means. Even if we know what the demand and supply are for a given product in a market environment, the price will keep moving up or down as the market determines. It will not stand still for much longer than a moment. Thus, the equilibrium price must be, at best, an approximation, meaning that if there is a "true" equilibrium price, the market price will only approach it, rarely attaining it.

Where the product or service has many different components or options, the price may represent a partial price, or it may be complete or incomplete, or it may be the price for the short run (for example, if it's on sale) or the long run. Thus, the price we see, even if it is the prevailing or predominant price across an economy, is only a result of the current ups and downs of many transactions and will not predominate long. As Thomas C. Schelling notes, unless someone is interested in *how* dust settles, he can simplify the analysis by concentrating on what happens after the dust settles. Thus, by looking at the price, we miss the process that made the price what it is.

Even if we could look at the equilibrium prices themselves, it doesn't mean we think that everything is settled and stable. We need to understand that the process that established the price involves people doing what they do, buying what they want and need, and reacting and *adapting* to what other people do and buy. So by looking at the results of theories based on assumptions that don't really reflect real behavior, at best, we end up describing a special case—equilibrium in this instance. We make the description our "normal" when, in fact, it is not really normal at all. Schilling gives a good example: There was a time when science believed that the planets revolved around the sun in circles. When astronomical observations showed that they did not, people asked, "Why not?" They tried to find what kept the planets from making circles. In the end, it was realized that in accordance with the laws of motion and gravitation, there had never been a reason to expect circles. Circles were not the norm; ellipses were. The same is true for equilibrium prices. We should not expect that the prices we see represent normal prices for the supply and demand of any given product or service.

The problem with "markets" is that we can make them work in our economic theories only by making some unrealistic assumptions. For example, we assume that people make rational decisions in buying what they buy. Rational decisions require information on which to base decisions, but as we've just seen, most of the information that is available is incomplete or biased in order to get us to buy the product or service. In addition, many buyers don't bother to read the information even if it's on the product when they buy it. Because we believe that there are laws to make the products safe and that companies have to tell the truth in their advertisements and labels, we take for granted that we're getting a good, safe product and that market competition is giving us a pretty good price. Thus, people lack the knowledge to understand what they are buying in many products, especially if technology, chemicals, or medicines are involved. We don't shop around as often as we could to compare prices and quality. The bottom line is thus that the assumption that rational consumers are buying what they want or need is, at best, fiction, because we end up buying various products because someone else bought it and we don't want to be different or to look like fools for buying the cheaper version or an off brand, or we do, in fact, buy the less expensive version in order to look wise. As we have seen, people have many motivations that have little to do with rational decision making.

The genius of a market economy is that it allows us to make things we want and need in quantities that generally match those wants and needs. Money, talent, labor, and natural resources are thus used more for things we want and need and are used much more efficiently than would happen in a planned economy. This also makes our economy more resilient in the face of business cycles and the shocks that occur from time to time. Resilience recognizes that we can't know or prevent all future dangers, so it gives us good reasons to develop systems that provide access to health care for everyone; to construct better transportation, water, sewer, and communication infrastructure; and to invest in truly excellent education systems not only because it is the right thing to do but also because it prepares us to deal with the unknown.

SPENDING

When we look at the aggregate economy, we are examining the behavior of everyone in that economy. As we have mentioned, for people to live in a prosperous, growing economy, GDP has to grow. Recall that GDP not only is the price we pay for all the final goods and services we make but also represents the total incomes we all make, so for GDP to grow, we must spend more. For the whole economy, this spending is called aggregate expenditures (AE). If the formula for GDP can be written as Y = C + I + G + NX, the formula for aggregate expenditures is similar and is written as AE = C + I + G + NX. It is not exactly the same, however. The difference is in the term for investment, I.

The aggregate-expenditures "I" refers to *planned* investment. What's the difference? Planned investment comprises the investments we make so that we have goods and services to sell in the future. Planned investment happens because businesses have to plan ahead to make the right amounts of goods and services to meet the demand they think they will have in the future. Most often, they do this by forecasting the levels of inventories they will need. Thus, much of planned investment involves the changes in inventory that is produced to fill future needs. If companies believe they will sell more products in the future, they invest more in their inventories; they make more products and probably hire more people to produce the goods and use more machines for longer periods of time. If they think they will sell fewer products, they cut back on production; inventories shrink, and fewer people and machines are used. When more people are working, earning more money, aggregate spending increases. The opposite is true when fewer people are working: aggregate spending decreases. Thus, the changes in economic activity can be explained by something occurring that is *unplanned* and thus causes firms to react by hiring or laying off workers and producing more or fewer products and services than they thought they would. What are these unexpected events? The standard theories say that they are shocks.

The more connected our world has become, the more surprises are caused by events we never knew would affect our firms. If we consider the formula Y = C + I + G + NX, we see that the things that change any of the components of the formula will change GDP. Once those changes reach some critical threshold of aggregate expenditures or aggregate demand for what the economy produces, we can see a business cycle starting, accelerating, slowing, or ending.

We don't just let changes to the components of GDP happen by themselves without some government action, however. That would be too much like a laissez faire economy with no real inputs or controls from government, a formula that has led to disaster in the past, so we try to predict what will happen in the economy and to use government fiscal and monetary policies to try to make the economy act the way we want. Although we have had some successes from time to time in changing the trajectory of the economy, we don't seem to be able to make the desired results last for long. Most often, we overshoot or undershoot our targets because we really don't know how much to change the money supply or regulations, how much the government's actions will change economic activity, or how long the changes will take to work. We also really don't know how close to the top or bottom of the business cycle we are. It takes too long to gather the information that can tell us any of these things. The economy is just too complex. When we change policies, the system adapts, like complex systems do, and we get surprises we hadn't counted on.

COMPLEXITY IN MONETARY POLICY

Let's look at money, an example of something that is as complex as the rest of the economy. The Federal Reserve (the Fed) has the authority and the tools to change key interest rates and the money supply. Banks can loan money only if they have it, but they can lend out only a portion of it, by law. The Fed establishes the percentage of reserves—deposits—that banks must retain and are not able to loan out. These limits are called "reserve requirements." Under current standards, most banks can loan out about 90% of their reserves. For each bank, the actual percentage of its deposits it has to hold in reserve varies from 0% to 10%. There is no reserve requirement for deposits from 0 up to $12.4 million; there is a 3% reserve requirement for the next deposits from $12.4 million to $79.5 million; and there is a 10% reserve requirement for deposits above $79.5 million.

From time to time, some borrowers don't make their payments on time, and the reserves make sure the bank has enough money on hand to conduct business (paying customers' checks and transfers). Just in the course of doing business, it sometimes happens that the banks need to increase their reserves to meet their reserve requirements. They can do this by borrowing money from the Fed at an interest rate called the "discount rate," although more often, they borrow from other banks at the "Fed funds rate," which the Fed also basically controls and which is usually the more important of the two rates. These loans can be quite large, but they are for very short terms of maybe a few hours or overnight. The discount rate and the Fed funds rate are the major ways the Fed establishes the interest rates that banks charge for their loans to customers and to other banks.

The Fed funds rate and discount rate also help establish the overall interest rates on savings in the economy. This means that if you are going to invest money, you will compare the rate of return you make on that investment with the rates of return on other investments. With this information of overall interest rates in the economy, the Fed can also change the money supply. It does this by buying and selling treasury bonds in the bond markets. When the Fed sells bonds in the market, which is called "open market operations," it decreases the money supply, because the banks, big investment funds, and individuals who buy the bonds pay their money to the Fed. Money thus leaves the economy and goes to the Fed. To increase the money supply, the Fed buys bonds in the market, paying money to banks and investors.

The interest rate that the government pays on these bonds is set by the market. The Fed has gotten very good at knowing just how many bonds to buy and sell to keep the right amount of money in the money supply. With too much money compared to GDP growth, we get inflation; with too little, we can get deflation. If GDP grows about 3% in normal times, the money supply will grow about 3% as well, and we have stability in our prices.

This is a balancing act, to be sure, because of the lag in getting numbers for the growth of GDP. The lag in information is often weeks long and means that the Fed and economists in government and academia don't know for some time if their changes in monetary policy worked. The bottom line is that it's hard to know until later how much money to add or take out of the economy and whether it worked.

Inflation plays a role in our efforts to predict the amount of money needed in the economy as well. If inflation in the United States is higher than in other countries, products in other countries will be cheaper and our consumers will buy the imports, so money flows out of the country and the money supply shrinks without the Fed doing a thing. If inflation is lower in the United States than overseas, people in their countries buy our products and money flows into our economy, increasing the money supply, again without the Fed having a hand in it. Because workers are paid to make the products we export, they have money to spend, but the products they might buy might have been sent overseas, so we would have the money coming in from overseas for our exports, our products going overseas, and workers with more money to spend, so there is upward pressure on prices and we have inflation. You can understand the pressure on the Fed to get it right, and the complexity of the system the Fed deals with.

A lot of very smart, experienced people spend a lot of time developing predictions and policy options, running them through computer simulations and calculations, trying to get the balance right. They watch what happens when they make changes to see how the economy responds and then learn what works and what doesn't. The next time they try those policies, however, even when the situation looks similar, they will get a different result because the system has adapted and changed just because the policies do, in fact, change things.

Complexity is being added by the evolution of new kinds of currency: money being created by communities of people and businesses. It's not counterfeiting, because they aren't trying to make anyone believe that the money they use is US dollars. There are a number of these complimentary money systems around the world, including in the United States. BerkShares is a local currency that started in the Berkshires region of Massachusetts. About 400 businesses in the area accept BerkShares the same as dollars. As of 2011, about 2.7 million BerkShares were in circulation, issued from 13 branch offices and participating banks. The BerkShares even have an exchange rate with US currency: 1 Berkshare = .95 USD. In Ithaca, New York, there is the HOUR, with an exchange rate of 1 HOUR equaling $10. The HOUR apparently is used to help stimulate local economic activity. Whether real or virtual, some of these currencies are used to pay for goods and services such as language classes, babysitting, computer support, home-cooked meals, and discounts at local businesses. In China, several local currencies have sprung up. One that became very popular was the MITBBS, which is a currency that exists only online and was started by an MIT graduate, Liu Jia. Virtual currencies became popular enough that the Chinese government issued rules to control virtual currencies in its market.

Complex systems create surprises not only in the way businesses are organized but also in how they make and receive payments. The tasks of the Fed, and government in general, to try to regulate or control economic and other activity are not going to get any easier over time.

MESSY BIG DATA

There has been growing interest in a subject called big data, which I mentioned in the previous chapter. With our modern ability to generate and use information from many sources, and the strength of our computers to find associations, make calculations, and help draw some conclusions, we are becoming better at making many kinds of predictions. Several books have been written on the topic of big data in the past ten years or so demonstrating successes in predicting a wide variety of topics such as stock prices, the spread of the flu, who will flunk out of college, and much more, including certain aspects of economics. V. Mayer-Schonberger and Kenneth Cukier have written a book titled *Big Data: A Revolution That Will Transform How We Live, Work, and Think*. They point out that the key to big data is that it is a way to find correlations. For example, Google predicted the spread of a new flu strain in 2009 called H1N1, a combination of bird flu and swine flu. By contrast, the information that was available to the Centers for Disease Control, the CDC, was weeks old by the time it was collected from doctors and clinics, and was only partial information anyway. By happenstance, a few weeks before the outbreak, Google had finished a correlation study relating searches done on Google and the spread of flu illnesses between 2003 and 2008. The searches did not focus on anything related to the flu or symptoms; it just found relationships between *any* searches on its search engine and the incidents of flu. These correlations between words, phrases, and topics with incidents of flu outbreaks resulting in predictions of where and when the flu would strike and what kinds of people were at risk turned out to be pretty accurate.

The point here is this: The kinds of searches and the topic being studied do not have to be related at all; there just has to be a correlation. Big data does not look for why there is a correlation; it only shows that there is one. For economics, the potential is clear. Collecting huge amounts of data can be done very quickly and the data can be very fresh. This has the potential of providing information to government and analysts within time frames that allow for more meaningful responses.

For example, PriceStats is a big-data project that spun off from MIT in response to how long it takes the Bureau of Labor Statistics (BLS) to gather and report information from 90 cities on 80,000 prices. PriceStats is able to follow 500,000 prices of products sold every day at a fraction of what it costs the BLS to gather its data, which are weeks old by the time they're available. Even if its data are "messy," lacking the absolute accuracy of typical BLS data, PriceStats data give a significant advantage to decision makers and is often more trusted than information developed by many countries outside the United States.

This has many potential benefits, but also many pitfalls, for economic analysis. Because the sheer volume of data being used is so great, we have some level of success in predictions, but we also lose exactitude—it can get "messy." However, the volume of data overwhelms the relatively few outlier data that the information includes. Also, with the huge amount of information used—an amount that will continue to increase at a staggering rate—there are privacy concerns about just how much information about individual spending habits, psychological profiles, job prospects, health, and much more should be available for analysis. In our everyday lives, we normally give companies, employers, and government enormous amounts of information, especially as we buy online. Our laws, however, were established for an analog world and most likely did not anticipate this kind of technology.

The implications for finding correlations in complex systems are important. Because it can look at such huge, messy databanks, big data is, in many ways, looking at data that mimics life. In other words, it appears to be a useful tool to examine complex adaptive systems. Because it does not require exactitude in the data to give useful results, big data is much faster and cheaper to use. The desire for specificity in data is an outgrowth of using smaller amounts of data than are now available. When the amount of data is smaller, we want to make sure it is accurate, and we also have the ability to make it more accurate when we select data that are directly pertinent to the issue we're studying. In contrast, with big data, the sheer amount of information makes the "messy" data of less importance, similar to the way that we have to limit the information that comes to us through our senses in order to make decisions and analyze what's going on around us. Finding cause and effect is another natural trait that humans have. When we find a correlation, we tend to automatically try to determine why the relationship exists. Big data and correlations don't do that. The results of big-data analysis may show the existence of relationships that might be topics for further study, but it only tells what exists, not why it exists.

Why do we think big data will change the way we think? That's a pretty big claim. Mayer-Schonberger and Cukier say that three types of companies have emerged from the use of big data. First are companies that have the data or have access to the data—all kinds of data. For example, Twitter has massive amounts of data about people flowing through its system: where they are, what they're doing, why they are doing it, what they're thinking, and much more. Many more companies have data on all kinds of topics.

Second are companies with the skills to use this data—consultancies, technology vendors, and analytics providers who have the special skills and knowledge to do the work. The skills and expertise are spreading as fast as the ideas for using the data.

Third are companies with the big-data mindset. More and more firms have founders, bosses, and employees with unique ideas about ways to discover and use forms of value. A company called Jetpac was started with data that most of us would never suspect has much value, using user-uploaded photos to make travel recommendations.

Big data is a relatively new field, but the technologies we use to collect and use data are progressing faster than we can imagine. This rapidly changing technology could be a giant piece of sand that rearranges the sand pile in dramatic ways. Its effects are difficult to predict, and it will require us to throw away much of our playbook and to think differently. It is unlikely that we can make rules fast enough to contain the possible directions that big data will take. We have to assume that more timely information will be available at some point. We also have to assume that the predictions will be better in some parts of the world than in others because methods of data collection vary and the accuracy of the data will vary as well. With the expanding power of our computers and networks, it is almost certain that our predictions will improve. For example, even though predicting behavior in many cultures is very difficult, so far, big data has been able to forecast what people do in many instances.

So how can we approach prediction and policy? The answer is that we have to think in a totally different way. We will still try to make predictions and policies, but we also have to change focus. The only way is to ask different questions.

If predictions and the policies change a complex system in surprising ways, we should ask how we can be more resilient. If resilience, rather than control of the system itself, is our goal, we are freed to actually *make the complex economy even more complex.* Why? Complexity, change, and surprising innovations are the engines behind economic growth. Resilience is that ability to bounce back and adjust, especially to negative events, that ability to cope with stress or adversity. You and I need to learn that we are not above the system but are part of it. We need to learn how to adapt to the rapid change that comes with an increasingly complex economy. When I say we should *allow* the system to be more complex, it is a recognition that the system is already more complex than we think; that's the normal state of the system—we just haven't discovered most of the complexity or taken advantage of it. Then, taking it from its normal level of complexity, we shouldn't be afraid to go further. How do we take advantage of this complexity?

PEER PRODUCTION

Yochai Benkler, a professor of law at the New York University School of Law, wrote an article for the *Yale Law Journal* in 2002 titled "Coase's Penguin, or Linux and the Nature of the Firm." In the article, he describes how in the past, we have looked at economic production either as employees in a firm following the directions of managers, or as individuals in the market following price signals. In recent years, however, another approach—peer production—has developed, having the potential to change everything, standing our assumptions, graphs, charts, and predictions on their respective heads. We will have to think in ways that are directly opposite of those assumptions if we are to explain the phenomenon of peer production.

The specific example used by Benkler to demonstrate this new way of thinking is known as free software or open-source software. As described by Benkler, free software

> "involves thousands or even tens of thousands of programmers contributing to large and small scale projects, where the central organizing principle is that the software remains free of most constraints on copying and use common to most proprietary materials. No one "owns" the software in the traditional sense of being able to command how it is used or developed, or to control its disposition." (abstract)

Not only is the software free of charge to anyone who chooses to use it, but none of the programmers are paid for their work, and anyone can add to or change the program. It sounds like an open invitation for sabotage, but that hasn't happened, because intentional sabotage and errors are repaired within minutes by one or more of the thousands of programmers developing the software. There is no central controlling group or person; it is an organic, adapting, complex system.

According to the abstract of Benkler's article, this method has systematic advantage over a hierarchical corporate-type structure. It also demonstrates the advantages of having the capital needed for production; computers and communications capabilities are widely spread instead of concentrated in the hands of a few. In essence, this mode of production is better than firms or markets because it is better at identifying and assigning human capital to the needed production processes, thus greatly reducing opportunity costs in that it loses less information about who is the best person for a particular job in the process. In addition, there are substantial increasing returns by allowing large clusters of contributors to interact with large clusters of information sources in search of new projects and collaborations. Also, removing property rights and contracts greatly reduces transaction costs of working with sources of information and collaborators and increases the return.

Joshua Ramo comments on how much excess capacity there is in the world economic system from unused ideas and misallocated savings, underemployed academics or researchers in countries where information is blocked. However, having excess capacity and unused ideas happens even in places where information is freely available but not accessed because business structures and practices limit our possibilities or direct us in ways that do not provide what the public wants or needs. Business structures try to sell us what they want to make and control both the supply and demand curves. Peer production not only drives the system toward its most efficient level but, in the process, also produces what we want and need, because we are the ones deciding what to make and how to make it.

From the standpoint of economics, peer producers work in ways that are opposite the assumptions made to make economic theories work. For example, peer producers tend to work for no financial reward. Hundreds of thousands of people provide sources of information to Wikipedia and quickly repair any sabotage that happens, according to a study by IBM. A 2005 study by the journal *Nature* favorably compared the accuracy of Wikipedia to that of the Encyclopedia Britannica, and subsequent articles in several medical and scientific fields comparing Wikipedia with peer-reviewed sources found its coverage to be of high quality. Apparently, contributions are done for the purpose of producing something that works well and is worthwhile. In essence, peer producers give their work and their product away for free, claiming no property rights.

Peer production also stands on its head the idea of a few people owning and controlling the most vital information needed to make a production process work. This kind of system also allows for some efficiency to be gained by spreading the work over a large number of people and allowing the best work to rise to the top as everyone checks each other's work constantly so that errors and sabotage are quickly corrected. In fact, the average time between sabotage and correction is now less than five minutes on Wikipedia. This system also puts to use the underutilized skills of many people whose contributions would be lost to a system controlled by a few. Think of the networks that are brought into the system by adding those people to the production of almost anything at little or no cost. With our rapidly developing communications systems, all of this is not only possible but becoming more probable all the time.

Economist Brian Arthur explained that the standard view of economics is that the economy is "mechanistic" in that it is made up of objects that have linkages between them so that the objects and the system are separate things existing together. Thus, the object is acted upon by forces in the system and reacts in "predictable" ways. By contrast, Arthur explains, in a complex system, "subjects and objects cannot be neatly separated. So the economy shows behavior that we can best describe as organic, rather than mechanistic" (p. 12). Thus, we cannot use the old tools to describe the economy's behavior. Ecologist C. S. Holling identified many systems that can handle surprises with ease (wild grasslands, futures markets, entrepreneurial businesses), but he also found systems that, in adapting to unexpected events, retained bad ideas. In these "maladaptive" systems, "any novelty is either smothered or its inventor rejected." Such systems look good for a while but are eventually doomed. They just can't shed their bad ideas fast enough to adapt successfully.

FORECASTS AND EXPECTATIONS

In many ways, we have had some success in making policy based on information gathered in our old ways. In the 2007–2009 recession, had the Federal Reserve and Treasury department not reacted by pumping hundreds of millions of dollars into the economy, we would have almost certainly collapsed into another Great Depression. Our current forecasts caused the Fed to keep interest rates low for several months after the "official" end to the recession in 2009. Those actions appear to have played a significant role, as the US economy has been making a slow, steady climb back to health. Even so, we will still have business cycles, recessions, and expansions in the future. Predicting them and reacting with the correct policies will still be difficult and will become more so as complexity and the effects of big data grow as well.

One of the problems with making predictions is that expectations can be created in various markets and change the course of economic activity. For example, one economic debate that has gone on for some years involves the relationship between inflation and unemployment. In 1958, New Zealand economist Alban William Phillips plotted 95 years of data in the United Kingdom showing the relationship between wage inflation and unemployment. The data seemed to show an inverse relationship; when inflation went up, unemployment went down, and vice versa. When he plotted the data on a graph with the inflation rate on the vertical axis and unemployment on the horizontal axis, the resulting line sloped downward to the right. The graph was named after him and is called the Phillips Curve. Although there was a lot of data to support the idea, there were also many exceptions. Basically, the curve seemed to describe a trade-off between inflation and unemployment in the short term. The relationship, however, did not hold in the long term. Why?

The cause, as explained by University of Chicago professor and Nobel Prize winner Milton Friedman, was the effect of expectations. The short-run trade-off existed, he said, but only because workers and firms sometimes expected the inflation rate to be either higher or lower than it turned out to be. The difference between the expected inflation rate and the actual rate could cause the unemployment rate to rise above or dip below the "natural" rate of unemployment. In aggregate economics, you may recall, in the long run, there is a maximum amount of output possible in the economy. At that point, all the factories and machines are producing all they can and every worker who can work is employed. At that point, there are still some people who are unemployed because they're looking for new jobs and some workers don't have the skills needed. Whatever that unemployment rate is, thought to be around 5%, is the natural rate of unemployment.

Now let's see how expectations derived from forecasts of inflation might change the economy. We'll use a wage negotiation for one company in this example, but you can see how it would work if several major companies followed suit, as they often do. Consider General Motors negotiating a wage contract with the United Auto Workers (UAW) union. There has been a forecast of a 5% inflation rate in the coming year. GM and the UAW are both interested in the real wage, which is the nominal wages adjusted for inflation. Now suppose they negotiate and sign a contract with wage set at $31.50 for the upcoming year. GM and the UAW believe the forecasts that there will be a 5% inflation rate next year. That means the real-wage rate for next year will be $30 ($31.50/1.05 = $30). Now suppose the inflation rate is actually lower than expected. If the inflation rate turns out to be 2%, the actual real wage would be $30.88, which is higher than GM and the UAW expected. With a high real wage, GM will hire fewer workers than it had planned. If the inflation rate turns out to be 8%, the actual real wage would be $29.17, which is lower than forecasted, and GM will hire more workers than planned. Especially in the auto industry, the other companies would probably follow the wage rates set by GM and the UAW in negotiating their contracts. Thus, Friedman notes, an increase in inflation actually increases employment (decreases unemployment) if the increase in inflation is *unexpected*. The effect of the forecast would be to change the system it was forecasting.

This is an economist's version of Heisenberg's uncertainty principle, a concept in quantum physics that says that you change the thing you are observing just by observing it. The way physicists work their way around the uncertainty principle is to create thought experiments based on observations of real interactions. The thought experiments are meant to prove or disprove interpretations concerning the observation of the behavior rather than trying an experiment on the issue.

In economics, we have a complex system that is constantly adapting to a rapidly changing environment. Obviously, it is an environment in which experimentation is not normally possible; therefore, the key is to understand the environment as much as the observed behavior. Without understanding how the environment is changing and affecting the individual parts of the economy, it is unlikely that our understanding will generate information or predictions of much value, sort of like the broken watch that is correct twice a day.

An approach that is used in physical sciences might have some application in economics. More specifically, it would be useful to collect additional and different data that more closely represent the real environment in which economies operate and develop new measures of activity as well as data that can augment the accuracy of those measures we already use. By its nature, the information need is long term, meaning that the time frames we consider are long enough for the economy to adopt the best available technology and use our financial, natural, and human resources at their most efficient and sustainable levels. The long run also assumes full employment and full utilization of our productive resources, factories, and machines.

Alternatively, in this new view of the long run, we need to include more components of the economy, or more specifically, more *detailed* information about the economic change, but also information about what *actually causes* the changes in economic activity. When public policies are put in place, such as changes in government taxation and spending, the reaction to those new policies is what actually causes changes in economic activity. As we mentioned before, government doesn't make much but rather has to buy most of the goods and services it provides from private-sector sources. Thus, changes in government taxation and spending, which take money out of or put money into the economy, cause some part of economic slowdown or expansion. As noted, however, how the private sector reacts to these changes is not always predictable because of the complexities of implementing policy and the even greater complexity of the private sector. So, how can we do better at both implementing and determining the effects of policy changes?

Instead of focusing on the big categories of economic activity only, the answer is to use our technology, our networks, and our developing knowledge of the complex economy to focus on the *actions of people*. We also have to understand that we will not be able to predict what those actions will be. If what we measure ends up being what we focus our attention on, this means that we should measure complexity and unpredictability! What I am proposing is that by measuring complexity, we will focus on policies that encourage complexity *and* on our ability to adapt—to be resilient. As I said, more complexity means more networks, more surprises in innovations, and more entrepreneurship. It drives the development of new ideas in addition to being able to react more quickly to the new ideas of others.

Marina Gorbis in *The Nature of the Future* notes that with networks adding economic value to the social value they were originally based on, we are moving away from the dominance of large organizations such as corporations, universities, banks, centralized government, and large charities, toward production of goods and services by social, commons-based, open-sourced peer production. The large organizations have been nodes through which resources have flowed. The Internet is no longer based on nodes through which data and information flow toward other nodes and destinations; it is now a "distributed" network of many nodes acting more like individuals. Information is broken into small, micro-sized packets and sent by different routes and reassembled at the destination. If one route breaks down, the information does not stop flowing but simply takes another route to the destination. Our social networks are similar. None of us has all the information about a topic, and often, the information flows to us from several directions, which is how ideas from many people in our complex networks come together in us to generate altogether new ideas. Some of those ideas in the heads of some people turn into activities that create value by using those same networks rather than forming corporations or giant new nodes.

The nineteenth century, it has been said, was the century of the great entrepreneurs—Rockefeller, Carnegie, Morgan, and others. The twentieth century was the century of the corporation. In the twenty-first century, we are moving beyond the corporation to something else—something that will focus on people.

CHAPTER 6

THE MAXIMUM SUSTAINABLE ECONOMY

Those who can't change their minds cannot change anything.

—George Bernard Shaw

What is the maximum sustainable economy? Can we really get to a point where there is predictable economic stability? Can we do it through public policy? Asking such questions opens doors that we have walked through before, but not in economics. Hopefully, we can learn from our experiences that complex systems cannot be dealt with by passing a few laws and setting up a commission or a new department of government. The actions we take will have to be complex and messy.

If we understand that we can't control the kind of growth we want, then our best approach is to create the environments in which increasingly complex systems are the norm. If we want more complexity, which creates more innovation and thus resilience, we need to look at the infrastructure required for such a world. There is another aspect of this infrastructure that may seem as counterintuitive as the idea of creating more complexity; this infrastructure cannot have geographic limits. If you try to fit complexity into a box defined by political borders such as cities, counties, states, or even countries, then you defeat complexity. The sand pile is bigger than any one location.

In the real world, we know that many places will not adopt these new ideas easily, or maybe at all. The level of complexity will not be evenly distributed, so we must build the infrastructure so that it can work with areas that have greater or lesser complexity. Even if a given jurisdiction puts in place all the policies and physical structures needed, the people living there still have to react and build the complex economic structure we're after, and some places will just be better or faster at it than others. Within the United States there are cultural, political, financial, and social differences between states and cities, let alone different regions of the country. Those states, cities, and regions have different histories and different ideas of right and wrong, wise and unwise, and acceptable and unacceptable. That is also what adds to complexity and adaptability: the ability to have differences working and trading with each other. The idea is not to limit differences and force them into the "box" of complexity but to develop the way they want and need to develop, which is hopefully different than any other place. We need to embrace these differences, not force them to be something they are not. That's the only way we will make this idea work. This means that there is no one type of infrastructure that will work in every place. Any new infrastructure has to be suited to the differences we find, meaning that the needs for new or different infrastructure must be decided by those who have to live with the infrastructure. The secret is to set up infrastructures so each community can change its own when it sees the need to change to adapt. Some communities may well want to lead change rather than react to it.

We must therefore keep in mind that this infrastructure is not meant to be a one-size-fits-all proposition. It is meant to allow change to occur not by force but by allowing the forces that cause change to have the option of working if they want to, and working in the best way they can wherever that change occurs. What we want to put in place are options, menus from which to select choices. This is how new ideas work. People come up with ideas in surprising ways; some ideas work, some don't. Over time, however, people get better at developing ideas, and change and adaptation become more efficient and create better options. Even the policy menus themselves will change as new ideas are developed and copied, or eliminated as the system evolves.

Here's an example of why ideas and change coming from within is crucial. Joshua Ramo tells of the effort to define how many fish can be taken from a given area without crossing some critical number that does not leave enough fish in the water to sustain the population of fish. In 1918, a Russian ecologist, F. I. Baranov, developed a mathematical formula to describe the problem. It was called the "catch equation." The idea became known as "maximum sustainable yield (MSY)." MSY thus reduced the problem to an equation. MSY said that if you carefully surveyed the area of water you were fishing, say a lake, and recorded the nutrients available, how fast fish bred, how many fish you had to begin with, and other variables, using the equation, you could calculate the natural "replacement rate" for the lake. The goal was to allow fishermen to harvest the maximum sustainable yield, and no more, if they wanted to keep fishing the lake for as long as they wanted. It sounded great. After a while, however, even after people followed the rules, instead of thriving, the fish started to die in massive numbers.

What was the problem? The complexity of the environment was so great and the relationships between each of the components in the environment so strong that, as C. S. Holling wrote (as quoted by Ramo), the "stability of a lake ecosystem can't possibly be reduced to a few variables" (p. 176). What you can easily measure in these complex systems matters less than what you cannot measure: the strength of the relationship between the different parts of the system. The complexity of the system, the mesh of interactions that make the system resilient, is what protects the system against the shocks that happen from time to time. The system adapts to shocks, like the shock of large numbers of fish being taken out of a lake over and over again. How strong these interrelationships in the system are, how fast the system can adapt, and how far the system can bend before it breaks define how resilient the system is. In the case of MSY, increasing fish harvests to MSY changed those relationships: more fishermen who didn't know or care about MSY may have come; more trash may have been left behind and blocked drainage channels, which wiped out the floating moss needed to feed the other fish that were a staple diet for the "target" fish. In this example, adaptation responses were produced not only in the lake but also by fishermen external to the studied environment. Who would have ever figured on increased foot traffic in developing the catch equation? Even though MSY proved to be deadly to fishing areas, it became the policy used by more and more ecosystem resource managers because they felt they were doing something "scientific." The catch equation made sense on paper.

Another interesting aspect of these complex systems is that what are most likely to cause big changes in the system are not fast-changing variables, such as number of fish caught in a day, but shifts in slow variables. Often, the changes we see as occurring fast are the result of longer-term changes in slow variables. Aside from MSY, shifts that appear to happen quickly and unexpectedly in fish populations may in fact be due to the slow rise in the temperature of the water. The things that are around us longer and change more slowly have the most profound impact on complex systems. Those are also the things we often ignore precisely because they do move so slowly. Thus, resilience may be the most difficult characteristic to figure out. We can run around chasing after fast-changing variables all day, but unless we understand the underlying slow forces, we will fail. If we are aware of the slow variables, we can learn to use the fast variables to make the system more adaptive, more resilient. In an environmental example, it would be like using fast controlled burns of underbrush in forests to help make the forest less prone to larger fires. Economist Raghuram Rajan faulted Federal Reserve Chairman Alan Greenspan for allowing only two mild recessions during his tenure. Rajan thinks we should have several "varied and preferable mild ones, so we can stress test our systems" (*Has Financial Development Made the World Riskier?*, NBER working paper, Oct. 2005).

The approach of the United States and most other countries, however, is to use "resistance" policies—trying to stop the fast variables. Resistance policies try to prepare for every possible emergency, which is, of course, impossible. The Department of Homeland Security mission is "deterrence, prevention, and preemption of and defense against, aggression." Interestingly, resilience is not part of the mission. Much of what we face cannot be predicted and thus prevented. Resilience would come in the form of better health care, better infrastructure, and better education systems. We should try to prevent what we can, but it is perhaps more important that we are able to bounce back quickly from and learn from the surprises, both negative and positive, that will happen. Government alone cannot build systems fast enough and flexible enough for the modern world. We need to use the even greater strengths and abilities of each of us.

This is why I say that to make a system more resilient, we need to broaden our approach, learn new skills, and gather different information in different ways, to get into those interrelationships in the *real* system to better understand what makes the system sustain *itself*, not impose "linear" external rules and procedures. Complex systems are full of parts that have different strengths and life spans that are not evenly distributed across the system. Government alone can never construct a system fast enough and flexible enough for our modern world.

We should begin with what can be done. We can start by asking the sorts of questions we CAN answer and control, reaching for the places where the slow variables of our society are within our reach: How do we consume? How do we educate our children? How do we run our businesses? How do we invest our money? How do we build our cities and move our stuff? How can we have good places to work and live? How can we be healthier and happier? In the end, government can't make our economy fully resilient. It's a process that has to include each of us. We have to be aware that the networks that tie us together also amplify disturbances and the more efficient the networks, the faster they spread the dangers. Those same networks, however, also offer the best possible way to transmit change for ideas and decency.

Ecologist C. S. Holling also studied maladaptive systems, which can't change or adjust fast enough to surprises. Systems can become maladaptive when we base our decisions on bad information or on old ideas. Such systems snap when they meet the real world, says Holling. Ecologists call it lock-in. Ramo suggests that successful resilient systems have the ability to constantly develop new concepts for problems, generate diverse ideas, communicate with everyone, encourage novelty, and maybe even encourage a revolt or crisis every now and then.

If we are going to ask different questions, and most likely get different answers, we will have to look in a different way at the functions that government performs. This will mean creating a different organizational chart and will most likely create different functions that are altogether new to public management. With each department, the functions will have to include the ability to innovate and to try new approaches to an ever-changing, complex economy. Within government, we will have to have public policy entrepreneurs, people who can look at new complex problems and develop perhaps radically new approaches to those problems. This will, in turn, require more involvement of citizens who have knowledge about, have experience with, or are affected by the problems that change creates in their parts of the economy, city, or state.

If we are to address the issues that emerge from the goals mentioned above, the thinking, processes, and policy-making procedures will have to be redone. It takes our federal, state, and local governments far too long to react, and the reaction, if it comes at all, is often far too late to make a difference. Thomas Friedman writes that he would like to be China for one day, but not two. By that, he means that China can make decisions very quickly and get things accomplished much faster than we can, so for maybe just one day, if we could do that, we might accomplish a lot, but he would not like to live under that system of government for more than a day. The ability to make fast decisions and implement them quickly is part of China's complex system that has allowed its rapid growth over the past 30 years. Without China's form of government, that rapid growth would not have been possible.

One of the prices we pay for a democratic republic is that it takes time to make and implement decisions. That's because of the process of public debate, public input, and open government. That's a trade-off worth the price, I'd say. Although China is growing faster than the United States, it is showing some strain—inflation, a rapidly aging population, rising wages and lower productivity, the effects of corruption and state-owned enterprises, and more. China is caught in old ideas of economics and governing and is trying to make those ideas work in a modern and complex changing world economy. I like the United States' odds better. We have ways to adapt, if only we'll seize the opportunities.

CULTURE

We will discuss the physical infrastructure needed for diversity and complexity later. In this section, we focus on the key element in the infrastructure of a society that is growing economically: the culture. There are places where change, outsiders, and "different" people are not welcome. Although this type of culture is part of a complex system we are describing, we want places where innovation and creativity occur. As we discussed a bit earlier, Richard Florida, in his seminal book *The Rise of the Creative Class,* describes the differences in various people-related "capital" that can exist in communities. Social capital includes the value of people working and living together: a version of teamwork. Although generally thought to be a good thing, social capital can also be a negative force. When people live and work together for long periods of time, they do develop into "teams" and can be more effective in many aspects of life. On the other side, they can also exclude "outsiders." They can develop their own ways of doing things, and their own beliefs about good and bad, wise and unwise, right and wrong can become chiseled in stone; thus, they become reluctant to change. Even the suggestion of doing or thinking differently may mean being disciplined by the group, maybe excluded.

In Florida's work, human capital refers to the skills, abilities, knowledge, and experience that people bring to the group or the task at hand. The human capital of each person is unique and will be expressed in different ways, but it adds value to the group and often adds to the human capital of others, making the group more capable of accomplishing any given set of tasks.

Creative capital is the use of human capital in new ways. It results from having insights, new ideas, and those a-ha moments that bring new ways of thinking to the group and to the tasks they perform or the way they think.

What Florida finds is that human capital and creative capital are strongly correlated with economic growth, which in turn is related to innovation. This relationship between innovation and economic growth is well documented. Florida also shows that social capital does not contribute to economic growth nearly as much as the other types of capital, because its value peaks when the value of teamwork has peaked but innovation is lacking. Thus, few new ideas and little change result from what has always been done before. Because human and creative capital are not evenly distributed across society, what Florida does, then, is to identify the kinds of communities that attract creative and human capital.

Examining the details of complex systems and the networks they include, we see that these networks are of two kinds: strong ties and weak ties, as we briefly discussed earlier.

The strong ties we have are with our families and closest friends. We know a great deal about them and share a great deal of our public and private lives with them. Statistically, we are able, on average, to have up to about ten or so people in our strong-ties networks. The weak ties we have are more like acquaintances than friends; although we may have contact with them on some regular basis, we otherwise have little occasion or desire to share much of our lives with them. As a result, we generally have very large weak-tie networks made up of those we meet through our work, organizations, neighborhood acquaintances, and other casual contacts. It is through our weak ties, however, that we more often find new jobs, share information, and send and receive new ideas. Thus, the spread of innovation happens much more frequently when there are people with more weak ties. What Florida reports is that innovation and creativity are highly correlated within areas of high weak-tie networks but are negatively correlated with areas of high strong-tie networks, those areas with high social capital.

This is not to say that social capital is not needed. It is. It is important in any community and helps provide definition and personality for communities. It is often part of what attracts people to certain cities and keeps them there, or in some cases drives them away. It helps absorb newcomers and provides some level of security and sense of belonging. Places such as Chicago, Seattle, and Minneapolis have strong doses of strong- and weak-tie networks. The goal is to understand the forces that are at work in any community and to use them to build cohesive, open, and tolerant places to live. Most often, these things evolve gradually as people move in and out. If social capital becomes the dominant factor in the community or neighborhood, that's when outsiders can't break in to the social fabric of the area. When human and creative capital dominate the community and social capital gives it flavor or personality, we find the possibility of growth.

While the communities that have low levels of creativity and innovation are also part of a complex system, those areas of high innovation and creativity are the ones that drive economic growth. Thus, it is not surprising that those high-growth areas also have high levels of income inequality, higher wages and hours worked, more diversity, more human capital, and more innovation. These characteristics seem to be both a cause and result of economic growth and prosperity.

Florida also sees these differences between communities with low levels of innovation and those with high levels of innovation as a possibly troubling trend: a divide in American society, as he describes it. Two distinct societies may be developing, with different institutions, different incomes, and different cultures. One is very diverse, educated, professional, creative, and urban, and less involved in politics. The other is more closely knit, more church-based, older, more civic-minded, blue-collar oriented, and rural in nature. The former group is becoming more dominant socially and economically while the latter is becoming fewer in number and has fewer economic resources. Part of the reason is that the areas that are more diverse are easier to enter, have more attractive amenities, and are places where newcomers are more easily accepted. The closely knit rural areas have fewer amenities and can often be less welcoming to newcomers.

MAKING COMPLEX COMMUNITIES

Several years ago, one of my jobs with the State of Indiana was to attract new jobs to the state. I quickly realized that new companies didn't locate in Indiana but located some *place* in Indiana, so my staff and I spent a great deal of time working in cities and towns to help them develop the physical and organizational infrastructures needed to be successful. In those days, economic development was focused on attracting big employers that would employ lots of people; thus, local communities focused their attention on the capabilities of their water and sewer systems, fire and police services, school systems, and transportation connections, and on improving their downtowns and shopping areas. Their idea was that if they could build the right things, they would attract jobs. For many communities, making these improvements did, in fact, help attract new employers and keep their existing ones from leaving, so our numbers looked very good statewide, with several really large successes.

Those days, however, are long gone. If you talk to employers today, you find that although these infrastructure items are important, all the places they would consider already have them. What is important now are things that are difficult to build by hiring contractors. What is important now is having the right people with the right skills, usually skills that involve technology and innovation in some way. Not only does a community have to have the right people and skills, the community has to be physically attractive.

This is a difficult standard to meet. A city can't just build a sports stadium or fix up its downtown. These things require a diverse place that has a variety of features that all sorts of people will like and want to have. In other words, it takes a diverse community, however you want to define "diverse." Recall that innovation requires lots of new ideas from people with different points of view, not one standard way of looking at things. The odds are that areas can't select the kinds of companies that will come looking at their communities. Cities and towns need to be able to be attractive to different kinds of companies and to the people who work at those companies. We're not just talking about communities with diverse skills, ethnic or racial backgrounds, or gender; we're also talking gay and straight, disabled and able-bodied. In other words, the community has to embrace *all* the people who come with being a truly diverse community.

If a community isn't like this, or is not even willing to try, in the long-run, it will not be competitive. This doesn't mean the community won't attract any new employers, just that it won't attract or keep as many as it could have. The employers that such a community attracts will more likely be those that do not need a diverse, creative workforce. In other words, they will not be firms that need innovation. While there will always be a growing economy in diverse and creative communities, there will always be those places that are culturally unable or unwilling to change as quickly. They may adapt over time, but they won't lead change. Eventually, their employers will have to adapt to new technologies and new management systems in order to be competitive. Because the staffs and employees of those employers will be drawn from those communities that like the status quo, however, they will be unable to change quickly.

Edward Glaeser in *Triumph of the City* writes that there might not be much cities can do to change their economic fates. Glaeser, a Harvard professor who studies urban economics, says that the success that cities have had in recent times is the result of decisions made years, perhaps centuries, ago, when the decisions were made about the locations and routes of transportation and which cities would be capitals or important ports. Those decisions not only put in place the infrastructure that was needed for certain kinds of economic activities but also brought to town more, or less, diverse populations that spurred more innovation, or not. Universities were founded, and trade with other nations and other parts of the country brought new ideas and money into some areas and not others. These things when present attracted people with various skills as well as entrepreneurs who took advantage of the resources available to them to prosper. Those skilled people and entrepreneurs then taught their children and friends how to do the same, and developing diversity and using economic resources became part of the culture. Other places developed other, less diverse, less innovative, less creative cultures with fewer ideas from the outside, and close-knit social capital dominated those areas while human and creative capital dominated the more diverse areas.

Those more diverse and less diverse cultures still dominate their respective areas today, according to Glaeser. For example, he points out that the relative education levels of cities in 1940 are highly correlated with the relative education levels today. If less than 5% of a city's population had a college education in 1940, then, on average, less than 19% of the population in 2000 had college degrees. In Indiana in 1940, 3.9% had a college degree (18% below the national average), and in 2000, the percentage was 19.4 (26%

below the national average). Today, a key to having a successful comeback or to start a new era in a community's economy is education, specifically a college education. Recent examples are New York, Boston, and Minneapolis, all of which fell on tough times in the 1960s and '70s but have since turned the corner into economic growth. Each also has a high portion of its population with college degrees: New York with 37% of its population, Boston with 39%, and Minneapolis with 37%. Indianapolis, by comparison, is at 25%, and Detroit comes in at 11%. If companies need innovation to prosper, the probabilities are that they will locate, expand, or stay in places with more college graduates and where learning and new ideas are part of the culture. In other words, companies want diverse economies with lots of networks with weak ties that bring in new ideas and people and keep them. It does little good to increase the number of people getting college degrees if there are no jobs requiring those degrees, however. Those newly educated citizens will eventually go looking for places to use their educations.

It also does little good to build physical assets such as sports stadiums, areas for great shopping, and theaters if the culture does not attract and welcome strangers. For a city to grow, it must attract money and people from outside its area. That's what growth is: more people and money. Nowadays, that means the right kind of people: educated; from different places, with diverse backgrounds; and with a drive to create, to imagine, and to find the tools to turn imaginings into realities.

If cities are going to try to change, they have to have integrated programs involving lots of people, companies, government at all levels, and idea people who can get things done. Successful change is not a matter of building or expanding education facilities; it is a matter of making a community that creative people want to come to, that has people like themselves and things for them all to do outside of work, things they like to do. That may mean things to do that are different from entertainment that's currently in the area. Communities need to see themselves through the eyes of those they want to attract. This can be difficult to do. It means having to start with a limited market for the shops, restaurants, shows, and places to hang out that are attractive to many kinds of people, so the hard starting point is with the people who live in town. That's why it's important to include people in the process—not just to get their input, but to also show them what is possible and that things will be not just okay but a really good change. Remember, we're changing a sand pile, not the surface the sand is on.

If lifestyle is important to the innovators, and it is, according to Florida and others, then let's look at some ideas that appear to work. Most cities have little money to make big changes in the physical infrastructure and to "reinvent" their downtowns or other parts of town. Even so, there are some changes in zoning and property tax laws that have motivated private developers to put time and money into various urban settings. Let's start with zoning.

MULTI-USE ZONING

Zoning causes us to have to drive. Zoning tells us where we can do certain activities and also what we can't do in those same areas. Thus, we can build homes in areas zoned for residential uses, but we can't have shops and businesses there. We can't build factories next to shopping centers if the zoning laws don't allow it. Thus, we have to drive from our homes to work or shop. That means not only more big roads and streets but more parking lots and garages; it means suburban sprawl because, most often, we can't build homes downtown or near our workplaces. Factories can't be built downtown, either, so they are most often built in suburban industrial parks far away from our homes and from where we shop. We've become used to such arrangements, so they seem normal and natural. We spend so much time in cars, subways, and trains that it's common to have commuting times of more than an hour in larger cities and of not much less time in medium-sized cities. Florida and Glaeser show that energy costs, pollution, loss of family time, and blood pressures are all up as a result. If we have to build cities so that those important activities have to be separated, what can be done? One answer is multi-use zoning.

Multi-use zoning allows more than one activity in an area. Its most successful use allows residential and commercial activity in the same areas, such as downtowns. Carmel, Indiana, is the poster child for multi-use zoning, and it is transforming its downtown. New condominiums are built with residential units upstairs and shops, restaurants, and offices on the ground floor. This arrangement allows people to live and work in the same area and, more importantly, gets them walking. People on foot make urban centers work. People in cars don't add to economic activity until they park their cars and become pedestrians. If people don't have to get in cars to shop, go to a play, or eat and can just sit in a nearby park and enjoy the sunshine, there's less need for wide streets, fewer cars speeding by, fewer parking lots and garages, and more commercial activity because there are more people on foot.

Jane Jacobs pointed out that under such circumstances, there is more "neighboring" going on, more watching out for each other. Merchants get to know the routines of their customers and of the people who walk past their stores; they see the same people doing similar things they do most days. They see the same kids going to and from school or to the movies at certain times and when the kids are doing things they shouldn't be doing, things you might want to tell the kids' parents about. Or the merchants might know when someone is hurting, has lost a job, is sick, or is worried about something, and they might help out. In such settings, innovators might also have lunch together, see each other more often, and make the quick date or appointment to do something fun or productive. One of the things that makes complex systems work is a high density of networks, where information is passed more quickly in many directions. This is more likely to happen in a multi-use zoning area than in a zoned-out typical urban setting. It is also a revival of the norm that existed as cities first developed, when people lived on the second and third floors above the shops and markets at street level. Factories were nearby, workers often walked home for lunch, and the people who ran those shops and markets did, in fact, recognize the routines of people who stopped in, walked by, or took time to rest on park benches, and they did try to keep the kids out of trouble. This is not a new idea, as Jacobs showed, but the way things used to be before society was overwhelmed by cars.

SITE VALUE TAXATION

Site value taxation is a shift in current views about property taxation. If we want cities and town to use multi-use zoning or to take their comprehensive plans (the technical name for the development plans for communities) off the shelf and put them to use, then site value taxation provides a strong incentive. In some states, including Indiana, it would probably take a change in the state constitution, but it at least needs a thorough public discussion. Basically, the idea works like this: Most property tax systems put the majority of the weight of the assessed value of a property on the structure built on the property and very little weight on the land. Thus, two similarly sized parcels of land in the same neighborhood would have different assessed values, and thus different tax bills, if one has a modest home built on it and the other has a larger, more elaborate home on it. We've become used to such a system, so it only seems right and fair. This system assumes that people with greater wealth will have larger, more expensive homes and should pay higher taxes. Site value taxation, however, looks at the situation in a different way. It places the bulk of the assessed value on the land and very little, if any, weight on the structure.

The value of land is related to its location relative to other development as well as to the nearness of public services such as utilities, fire hydrants, roads, and streets. Thus, undeveloped farmland has less value than land in the downtown of a city. Under site value taxation, the government would receive the same amount of tax revenue, but that amount would be based on the value of land in its jurisdiction. As you can see, the taxes on the land portion of assessed valuation would increase a great deal and the portion of the tax based on any structures on the land would fall to a very low number. The effect is to give people a motive to use the commercial and industrial land more intensely, to build bigger, better, and/or more valuable buildings in order to make money to pay the tax on the land, but the owners are not penalized for doing so. In fact, if the owners build or renovate buildings that produce more income, they get to keep more of it because their property tax bills would change very little and thus their profits would increase. In this way, unused or underused land is put to higher use. Owners of vacant properties, especially in urban areas, are motivated to put the property to use but are not penalized for doing so. When the changes in taxes paid on land and structures are calculated in most cities, we find that site value taxation would change residential and farmland total tax bills very little. If there are no improvements on farmland, there would already be no tax on a structure and the tax bill would not change. In most residential areas, the tax increases on land are pretty much offset by the decrease in taxes on residential structures. Under site value taxation, we would have the private sector building the buildings and paying for improvements. Under the current system, often, state or local governments have to give tax incentives to encourage private development, especially in industrial areas.

Site value taxation has been tried in various ways. For example, the effect can be created not by changing tax rates but by assessing the values of land and buildings to produce similar results. When site value taxation was allowed to work, development was accelerated in places such as Sydney, Australia; Fairhope, Alabama; and Southfield, Michigan. The development in the areas where the effect was used was noticeably different than in adjacent areas.

The heart of multi-use zoning and site value taxation (and there are hundreds more and better ones) is to increase the diversity of cities and networks and to have the private sector foot the bill because it wants to. Government should be a partner that uses its ability to tax and regulate as incentives rather than replacements for private investment. Government plays its best role when it provides what the private sector cannot provide or when the market fails or is insufficient for the activities that are needed. This role is most effective in an environment that produces new ideas and new products in cities with creative cultures. In *The Death and Life of Great American Cities,* Jane Jacobs wrote, "By its nature, the metropolis provides what otherwise could only be given by traveling; namely, the strange." Strange is a relative term, and Jacobs's meaning is that cities provide the unexpected new experiences that generate new ideas. The cities that do this best are those that are growing, adding new buildings, businesses, art, technology, and things that at first seem strange and later become the norm, like plows instead of hand tools and computer cell phones instead of main frames in air-conditioned rooms. Government can make economic growth happen better and faster if it plays its role as a partner with the private sector.

The economic system is complex, however, and is more than just improving education systems and having a culture of innovation and high-tech industries. Researchers have also found that real estate prices have a lot to do with diversity and growth. As we all can guess, those places that are growing are attracting more people than those places that don't grow. The education, diversity, and creativity of the growing cities is a stark contrast with those that are not growing. Because population growth occurs before housing stock grows, the prices of housing in growing areas is almost always higher as well. Thus, what develops is a phenomenon in which a vibrant labor market means higher wages as well as higher housing costs. On average, Americans spend about 40% of their incomes on housing, which means that as incomes rise with education and skill, the housing prices rise in those cities with educated and skilled labor. This in turn means that the 70% of the households with homeowners, as opposed to renters, make more money not just from their jobs but also because they live in markets that are growing. The renters, in contrast, may make more money than they would in other cities, but they are not making money from the rising values of owning property. In fact, they are transferring some of their wealth to the owners of the properties they rent, thereby increasing the discrepancy in incomes of areas. Low-growth regions have more renters; lower incomes generally mean more renters and an even greater disparity in incomes.

What this all means is that where we see higher real estate prices, we will most often, but not always (think Las Vegas), see more diverse networks made up of people with more education and skill levels and, most often, more innovation.

Interestingly, according to Edward Glaeser, where we see growing cities, we will usually see poor areas of the cities. Why? Most people move for economic reasons, meaning they are moving from situations that include having lower incomes to situations that include higher incomes. Still, until they make those higher incomes, those people who move have to live somewhere. Glaeser noted that a look at the demographics of poor neighborhoods shows that many of the people who live there move out within about five years and move to better neighborhoods. Thus, if a city does not have poorer neighborhoods, it is probably not growing—people are not coming to town for better job opportunities. If there are fewer or smaller poor areas of town, then the people who move in already have good incomes and have probably been recruited or are moving from one good job to another. If there are fewer high-income neighborhoods and very large poorer areas, then few people are moving to town at all because there are few new job opportunities for higher-paying jobs. Thus, the networks are made up of less diverse and innovative members.

The movement of people for higher-paying jobs is becoming international and often includes not just physically moving to another city or part of the world but also earning money in other locations through the "virtual" companies that do business online. The presence of virtual companies requires that innovation be present as well, usually at both ends of the line. If we look at Internet usage, Asia (mostly China) leads the way with 44% of the total users of the Internet, then comes Europe with 23%. North America has about 13% of the Internet users. These percentages are obviously related to population, but they show that a big portion of Internet usage is driven by Asian users. If we look at the penetration of the Internet in various region of the world, we see that North America leads the way at 78%, followed by Oceania/Australia at 60% and Europe at about 58%. Asia is at 24%, which tells us that if Asia's Internet usage is big now, we will see a much larger usage in Asia as penetration increases with economic development. Even Africa is at 11% penetration, which is leading to economic growth in many of its poorest regions, often because of buying and selling products and services using cell phones.

Thus, we can easily see how dense networks of tech-savvy people are coming together all over the world and creating ideas that could never have happened any other way.

CHAPTER 7

WHAT TO DO

Never confuse movement with action.

—Ernest Hemingway

We've taken a journey through some pretty strange places involving sand piles, complex systems, networks, and chaos. We have worked our way through cities, or, more accurately, through the tip of the huge "city" iceberg, and a few ideas have been offered along the way. In the end, what I am proposing is that we can't predict what will happen and that we should make prediction even more difficult by making things more complex than they already are.

Actually, if you look at it differently, the concepts I've proposed can change things so that they produce more than *can* and maybe *should* be predicted. What I mean is this: The world that has evolved has become more connected than ever before, creating a dizzying complexity that generates more ideas and brings more people into the equation than ever before. It will continue to become even more complex. What that means for each of us is that we are in *the* conversation; we can be actors that produce change. We used to live in a world where it took great people working in great organizations with great wealth to affect change. That world, though it still exists, is no longer the only game in town. The sand pile we live in reacts to large *and* small changes, for good or ill. Those changes and new ideas can come from Washington, Indiana, just as easily as they can from Washington, DC. They can begin in the South Side Vacuum Cleaner Company in Fort Wayne and have the same effect as if they came from Apple in Palo Alto. The key is to understand that this isn't just possible but is already the way things are. We have to adjust our thinking about what can be done, how it might be done, and who could possibly do it, because in such a world, somebody will, in fact, do it sooner or later. The charge we have is to rethink our way of encouraging the good ideas, our way of keeping things organized, regulated, enforced, and our way of implementing our ideas.

The way we have organized our governments and our companies was developed hundreds of years ago, and those entities are no longer up to the task of dealing with quick, continuous, unexpected change. The times have changed, and we have to think in different ways, free of the fear of hearing "we can't do that" or "we've already done that" or "that will never work." We cannot be sure of what will work and what won't, so we have to keep trying. We have to shed our fear of and our tendency to criticize failure or only partial success. Although we might feel that the world we are trying to change is too big and that only big things can make a difference, to think so is *the* mistake of our times. It is precisely opposite of the truth. As we have seen, it is the little things, the unexpected, the unknown ideas and events that can and often do make great changes. That is why we must all get involved. More to the truth of the matter, we are all already involved as we adapt to the newly connected world. As Joshua Ramo pointed out, change isn't something that is going to feel far away from us; it is something that is going to infect every part of our lives.

CAN WE CREATE INNOVATIVE ECONOMIES?

If we are going to increase complexity in our economy, it will almost certainly first happen in cities. David Banks at Duke University posed the question of why there were periods in history when concentrations of genius occurred. Examples are Athens from about 440 BCE to about 380 BCE, Florence from 1440 to 1490, and London from 1570 to 1640. These were the times of the great classical philosophers (Plato, Socrates, Euripides, Aristophanes, and more) as well as the great artistic geniuses (Michelangelo, Da Vinci, Bernini, and many more) and the great writers (Shakespeare, Marlowe, Raleigh, Bacon, etc.). Banks titled his paper on this topic "The Problem of Excess Genius." He looked at the usual explanations of prosperity, peace, freedom, social mobility, and new paradigm shifts bringing new ideas and tools into the mix, but he dismissed them all upon examination. In the end, he could find no satisfactory explanation.

Jonah Lehrer of *Wired Science* wrote an article in 2012 about the topic and found some common threads in these concentrations of genius in "the benefit of human mixing," by which he means cities, gatherings of many diverse people, the importance of education, and the development of institutions that encourage risk taking.

Stephen Smith, the founder and CEO of JogNog.com, points out that Banks's and Lehrer's conclusions were pointing toward three topics: the societies had recently achieved military victories, the societies provided places and processes whereby geniuses could share and debate new ideas, and the education systems encouraged one-on-one tutoring.

Lehrer, in his book *Imagine,* looks more deeply into the subject and finds that in those times, there were distinct changes in the cultures. He says, "Shakespeare was saved by his time." He points out that London had become obsessed with the theater and provided a living for creative minds like Shakespeare and Marlowe. Although many people have accused Shakespeare of plagiarizing ideas and story lines, the point is that there were other writers writing things worth stealing, something that had not existed before in England. "Elizabethan England proved to be the ideal place for a young dramatist to develop," (p. 127) Lehrer writes.

Paul Romer, an economist who in 1990 developed a new economic growth theory called Endogenous Growth Theory, writes that "ideas are an inexhaustible resource." He says that ideas inspire new ideas. That's why places that create new ideas show more growth than those places that don't: "When ideas are shared the possibilities do not add up. *They multiply*"" ("Endogenous Technological Change," *Journal of Political Economy,* Oct. 1990, pp. S71-S107; emphasis in the original). Growth takes more than people, however. There are plenty of examples of large cities that don't create innovation or grow. Such innovation and growth require a place where the costs of density of the population don't outweigh the benefits. The key is not that talent and intellect aren't found everywhere but that only some places take advantage of the talent and intellect through their rules, institutions, and cultures. During the time of Elizabeth I, there was a relaxation of the censorship laws; Shakespeare could then create his plays with little fear of being jailed. During this time, education became more generally available, and even though Shakespeare's father was barely literate, William was able to attend the free Stratford grammar school at the age of seven. These free schools supported the development of London's literary talent and allowed Shakespeare and others to learn from each other and to share or steal worthwhile ideas. Romer also tells of T. S. Eliot writing, "The great ages did not probably produce much more talent than ours. But less talent was wasted."

The United States has become the driving force of much of the world's economy. Although most people believe that our huge consumer markets and advanced manufacturing prowess are at the heart of US strength, they would be wrong. The United States' biggest export is technology and innovation. Our need for ideas is so great that we rely on immigration to supply us with enough scientists and engineers to supply the needs we have. The immigrants come because we are probably the most open country in the world, a place where highly skilled people can come and fit in pretty quickly. The opportunities are not evenly distributed across the United States, which implies that there are many places where people with talent will "cluster" with others who are similarly skilled. San Francisco, Austin, Minneapolis, Seattle, Chicago, New York, Washington, DC, Boston, and other innovative cities are what Bill Gates calls "IQ magnets." The United States is not the only place on Earth where these clusters exist, and many other parts of the world are working hard to attract and keep the talent they need to grow their economies. With competition comes the need to look at ourselves and evaluate what will keep us at the head of the pack, or at least able to compete.

According to Richard Florida in *The Flight of the Creative Class,* these clusters of creative people are concentrating in 20 or 25 mega-regions around the world. Florida has spent a great deal of time trying to figure out why this is and what makes these regions so attractive. At the heart of what he has found is the openness of society: openness to people of all backgrounds and to new and different ideas. This openness does not exist in many parts of the world. This has meant a worldwide migration of talent from countries where ideas and openness are restricted to those countries where they are embraced. Not surprisingly, the competition for talent is heating up. The United States has been the dominant player in developing and attracting talent for many years. Immigrants have been an essential part of the growth of our economy, as they are from diverse backgrounds and have learned different ways to think about problems and solutions. Hundreds of the companies in Silicon Valley were founded by immigrants, and most of the patents generated there have been awarded to engineers and scientists from elsewhere, patents that have created tens of thousands of jobs in the United States. The heads of many US technology and large manufacturing companies are foreign-born. This is not a recent phenomenon; it's the way it's always been. We can no longer count on that advantage, however, and much of our vulnerability in keeping and attracting talent is of our own making.

Other nations have long since figured out that openness and diversity are essential for economic growth and are making moves in that direction to create more complex economies. As mentioned briefly before, the Observatory of Economic Complexity, which is part of the Center for International Development at Harvard University, has developed the Atlas of Economic Complexity, which measures the economic complexity of 123 nations. At the top of the list is Japan, followed by Germany, Switzerland, Sweden, and Austria. The United States comes in at 13, right behind South Korea and ahead of Hungary. Mexico is 20th, China 29th, and Canada 41st in the rankings. Although this is not an exact correlation, the more complex economies tend also be the largest when measured by GDP per capita.

When Richard Florida compares the creative-class portion of workforces in countries where data is available, he finds that the United States ranks 11th. Much of the rest of the world is becoming more creative and innovative, as well. That means more competition for talent, both domestically and abroad. It also signals increasing complexity. It indicates that times are changing. More countries are opening up to new ideas. As the old-style communism faded away, places like Russia and China changed their systems, now allowing and often encouraging collaborations with Western scientists, engineers, medical researchers, and, as we see in the news regularly, astronauts. Complexity is spreading. The trick for many of the newly open societies will be to develop ways to cope with rapid change. That will be a change in culture and politics for some. Although China puts on a good show of having an open market economy, the reality is somewhat different. Its government is still involved in state capitalism and controls many of the major industries, with profits feeding the nation's sovereign wealth funds. China has favored industries and companies that have a better time of getting money and government support. The country is, however, more open than it was in the past. The government is working hard to develop the nation's university systems and is producing more and more scientists, engineers, economists, and mathematicians. The government is also collaborating with universities around the world in many forms, from curriculum development to basic research. Regardless of what you might think about the quality and number of creative-class members in China and elsewhere, their quality and complexity is increasing.

Even the United States' innovative growth is dependent on foreign talent. More than 25% of all of our scientists and engineers, nearly half of our engineering professors, and most of our PhDs in engineering, computer science, and life science come from foreign countries. As our existing workforce ages and retires, we will depend even more on foreign talent to fill the jobs they leave, because we do not have nearly enough technical talent in our high schools and colleges to replace them. By 2018, we will need three million more college graduates for all kinds of jobs than we will produce. We know this because we can count the people already in our schools who will have graduated by then. The only way for our companies and governments to find this talent is to look overseas. Naturally, this will increase complexity both here and abroad.

Even the number of foreign students in our colleges has continued to increase. In 2012, 764,321 foreign students were enrolled in US colleges—an increase of 5.7% from 2011. These students contribute more than $21.8 billion to the American economy aside from the effect they will have on job creation as they make their way into the workforce both here and abroad as the multiplier effect works its magic, creating, on average, 2.5 times as many jobs.

The multiplier is different for different kinds of industries and may be increasing as innovation spreads the effects of new technologies into all industrial categories more quickly, more often, and with greater impacts. Even so, we can't count on this flow of talent forever. Many countries are opening up and realizing that advanced education is going to be needed. Thus, they are expanding their post-secondary education programs rapidly and are collaborating with US colleges to do so. My teaching at two colleges in China has shown me how serious China is about reaching more students and building a college and university system that is competitive. With a middle class developing in many of these countries, students in these countries will not have to come to the United States for their educations as often, and those who do can begin going home to use their skills and knowledge. As Richard Florida writes in *The Flight of the Creative Class*, "The key factor of the global economy is no longer goods, services, or the flows of capital, but the competition for people" (p. 16).

What is developing are groups of cities that Florida calls mega-cities that are driving innovation and are likewise attracting lots of talent. The top tier includes New York, London, Tokyo, and Paris. Close behind are Chicago, Los Angeles, Frankfort, Hong Kong, Milan, and Singapore. There are second- and third-tier cities that are also hubs in this innovation-talent system, and Florida, in other writings, forecasts the development of more mega-regions on the horizon as these cities become more connected economically and technologically with other cities, forming entire large regions of innovation and talent. For example, as discussed earlier, one region stretches from New York City to south of Washington, DC, and another from about Pittsburgh westward to Detroit and Chicago. These mega-regions are developing in Europe and Asia, including India. Still, many places are not in mega-regions and will be at a disadvantage in attracting the talent, infrastructure, and money needed to succeed in the increasingly complex economy.

If we think of diversity in a global sense, we see that a city or region with many immigrants is not only more diverse but also more open to different ideas. The caveat to this is that the immigrants should come from many varied home countries rather than heavily representing one or two areas. For example, the city that has the most immigrants is Dubai, with about 82% of its residents being foreign nationals. Most of them (61%), however, are from India and Pakistan. Similarly, more than half of Miami's population is made up of immigrants, but most are from Cuba and Latin America. Amsterdam, Toronto,

Vancouver, Aukland, and Geneva have much more diversity among their substantial numbers of foreign residents. The Canadian cities will be especially strong challengers to the mega-US regions. It's not that Dubai and Miami will not succeed but that in the competition for talent that turns out innovation, other cities may have an even stronger advantage. These cities with more diversity among their immigrants offer top-class talent very attractive lifestyles along with the open diversity that encourages them to develop new ideas.

Statistically, the United States has an uphill battle ahead if it is to gain momentum. With more than 15,000 school districts across the country, each run by a school board made up of locally elected citizens, it would be by luck that many of those board members had any significant experience or training in developing and implementing education policies that can compete with school systems the likes of Shanghai's, generally considered the best in the world. There's a saying in sports that you are what your record says you are. In the case of education, the US is not meeting the competition. As mentioned earlier, we seem to be developing two societies: one urban, diverse, and educated, and the other rural, close-knit, and less educated. The former has more economic resources, and the latter has fewer. Those urban areas are more attractive and more diverse because they are not as closely knit as rural areas, are generally more welcoming to newcomers, and therefore grow faster. They are more diverse. Most of the United States' 15,000 school districts are in rural areas.

POLITICS IS A COMPLEX SYSTEM, TOO

Addressing these increasingly complex issues such as immigration and education as well as many new and surprising issues takes new directions in public policy, meaning politics. Politics is a complex system itself, however. Two basic truisms dominate our political institutions. The first is that important things happen in small rooms and unimportant things happen in large rooms; the second is that public policy is made by those who show up. The voting, speeches, public meetings, and press conferences that happen in big rooms are the result of meetings, strategies, and plans developed by people meeting in small rooms. Most often, those people, the ones who show up, do not include members of the general public. They include public officials meeting with their staffs, lobbyists, and public-interest groups to craft laws and policies that guarantee their continuation in power. Rarely do public meetings do much more than fulfill requirements for public "input" that most often has limited effect on the development of policy. Thus, there is a growing separation between the public and those who make the rules and policies. From time to time, policy makers go too far left or right in the public's eyes and we have a backlash at the polls. For example, the Newt Gingrich "Contract with America" conservatism was a backlash resulting from the election of President Clinton and his moves to get healthcare reform passed with his wife, Hillary, leading the effort. More recently, the rise of the Tea Party conservatives is, at least in part, a reaction to the election of President Obama and to the "bailout" of the banks and the auto industry. Each of those backlashes saw the pendulum swing back to the left as voters saw a lack of cooperation and compromise in Congress, and times of moderation broke out.

In the real world, the policies themselves often do not match the desires of citizens, as expressed in the Poling on issues such as gun control, healthcare, and immigration (legal and illegal). Even the question of whether the government can pay its bills (the debt ceiling) has been used as a weapon to gain political advantage in Congress. Polling has consistently shown that members of both parties wanted compromise among their representatives but those representatives instead stuck to "principles" that they were later willing to compromise only when they saw they were losing votes.

Thus, political decisions are also part of a complex adaptive system, making prediction of questionable value. Why? Predictions of losing votes often cause politicians to adapt and to change their positions. It is not possible to determine ahead of time what responses politicians will have to the ideas and pressures of lobbyists, contributors, and constituents, let alone the input from their staffs and any outside experts who weigh in. All of the inputs that public officials receive involve individuals each developing their own ideas and strategies that might change under only slightly different circumstances. On top of that, the public official filters those inputs through his or her own personality, experience, and points of view. Two officials would likely have different responses to the same information. Thus, public policy, fiscal policy, and the methods of implementing those policies are not as predictable as we'd wish.

Politicians, like the rest of us, respond to an environment that consists of people responding to *their* environment, which consists of people responding to an environment of people's responses, to borrow a phrase of Thomas Schelling. When our behavior depends on the choices other people make, there are no real options for prediction. This is especially true because we have incomplete information about what other people are doing, even among our friends or those around us. What are the odds that we'll be able to predict what politicians will come up with? Nate Silver's book, *The Signal and the Noise,* reports that even experienced political "experts" are not much better at making these kinds of predictions than you or I would be by flipping a coin. Those experts also attempt to influence public opinion, stating their positions as though they were objective truth rather than opinions most often reflecting a partisan bias. Even polling information is often gathered to demonstrate support or lack of support for what turns out to be a biased point of view or is presented in ways that "spin" the results one way or another.

In a public policy course I teach at Indiana University, I often poll my students on how involved they or their families have ever been in public affairs. Over the years, I have had only a handful of students who have ever attended a public meeting of any kind, written a letter or sent an e-mail to a public official, or even talked to friends about public issues. Many don't know their elected representatives and officials. As we study the US Constitution, I eventually come back to the results of the survey and tell them that for our current system to work, we should consider the First Amendment, regarding freedom of speech, not so much a right as a responsibility. If we aren't aware of what the government is doing and who we elect and don't tell them what we think, these public officials, who are not experts in most of the issues they have to address, have to do something and will pay attention to those people who *do* show up—lobbyists, business interests, special-interest and cause groups, academics, and so on. Thus, if we show up, we also have to show up informed. "You stink" does not help a public official much in knowing what to do.

This criticism may be unfair in some ways, because the complex nature of politics and the issues involved are difficult for many citizens to understand. Although local issues are complex, they can often be affected more by citizen input and involvement and often have a more noticeable effect on daily life than state and national issues, and local government can more easily receive input than can state and national governments.

In my time helping state and local governments attract investments that create jobs, and now as a teacher, I've seen many people go from the unemployment line to the line applying for jobs. I've also noticed many people moving from job to job many times, searching for something better. Part of the reason for their continued searching is that they don't really know what they want from their jobs. Most people will say they want a good paycheck and job security. Even so, many people who have those things are still searching because they are not happy and something inside is not being satisfied. In addition, most of those who feel that way have not taken the time to figure out what they want. We know from studies of happiness that money can provide happiness only up to a certain point. Beyond that point, the things that make us happy start becoming more individual but often include creating something new or doing something important to us, like helping others sacrificially, not looking for anything in return. The list can be as diverse as the number of people answering the question.

The reason many of the cities we have looked at are so popular is that they provide more opportunities not only for jobs, but also to find our own routes to job or life satisfaction, whatever that means to each of us. Sometimes, satisfaction means moving away from a current environment where we feel trapped or restricted in some way. Whatever is required, many of us keep searching until we either find it or give up and just accept our fate. I once heard a man say that retirement was his time to finally do what *he* wanted to do.

Our world now provides many more options for literally billions of people who never had options before. Not only does the Internet mean that we have more and more people becoming more comfortable using its power, but it is bringing online about 3 billion new consumers and more jobs than ever in human history. The very existence of the Internet means that people all over the world are seeing and experiencing things they never before knew existed and are forging changes in their governments and societies to make those things available. The genie is out of the bottle and cannot be put back in. There will be unexpected ups and downs from now on, and the best way to prosper is to learn how to adapt to surprise quickly; otherwise, we'll be left in the dust.

The role of government is changing. Government will have to be more responsive, because governments must provide the environments in which economies work. Government has to make rules that give incentives to innovate as well as to adapt to innovation. Those places with governments that make such an environment will prosper. Those that don't cannot.

I find that the government isn't always part of the problem or the solution. Over time, governments at all levels have often taken on roles that they are ill suited to perform. Although government does have a role in guiding parts of the economy and in providing for the health and safety of citizens, it cannot remake our culture. Because of residency requirements, government is a reflection of us because those we elect and appoint largely come from among us. If we are to become more innovative and complex, it will happen only as we change ourselves. Those kinds of changes happen over time, sometimes because of significant events. Mao tried to change culture in China—twice, with the Cultural Revolution and the Great Leap Forward—and all the Chinese got was poverty and heartache. China changed when the people were given encouragement by government, but it changed in a way that took advantage of the strengths that its culture already possessed. There will be resistance to change along the way; it's in our nature. Still, change will happen. Each succeeding generation is different from its predecessor, and this next one has many more amazing tools, more complexity, and more networks to accomplish the task. Government and the current generation just have to get out of the way and let new types of businesses, government, and cultures happen.

Evolutionary biologists Stephen Jay Gould and Niles Elderidge believed that new species mostly likely will develop at the fringes of a population, where small groups can become separated from the main body and then undergo changes that can give them a survival advantage over the dominant group. This new group will then eventually replace the dominant group members, not in a smooth transition, but in what they called a "punctuated equilibrium," as the stronger traits for survival gradually become dominant. We are in such a time of punctuated equilibrium with a new kind of economy that reflects a changing culture, a new way of thinking about how to get things done. We will need new ways to measure what's happening.

CHAPTER 8

AS WE ALL KNOW, CHANGE IS BAD

Coming back to where you started is not the same as never leaving.

—Terry Pratchett, *A Hat Full of Sky*

The next twenty to thirty years will see more change than the previous three hundred did. It will take speed and skill for people to cope. The ideas and technology we marvel at today will be the old ways ten years from now as new ideas and technologies take their place at a faster and faster pace. Individually, we will be able to see things change around us more quickly than our current organizations can respond. What needs to occur, what is essential, is that we change the culture and ways of thinking in our businesses, government, not-for-profits, and organized religion. That means developing ways to encourage skeptical critical thinking, as well as questioning fundamental beliefs and methods. Our core beliefs about morality and ethics do not have to change as much as the way we adapt to change.

I teach a course in organizational behavior at the University of Indianapolis. In it, we examine group psychology, how people behave, and what motivates them. There are many ways of describing how we do things together. One way uses the “three Ps” of psychology, politics, and pay as a way to organize thinking about decision making. Part of this approach looks at the biases we have that lead away from good decisions. Behavioral psychologists call this “status quo bias.”

In one example, people were given a large sum of hypothetical money to invest. Some were given money that was in low-risk, low-return bonds. Others got their money in riskier stocks and securities. Even though each group was given the option and some incentive to change its investments, both groups decided to leave their investment portfolios alone; thus, the investments they initially received governed the outcome of the test, rather than any of their own feelings toward risk or various investment instruments. People like to leave things the way they are. We have a fear of losing or of making mistakes, especially in the eyes of others. This type of behavior is often called an "external locus of control." People with this point of view feel they are victims of circumstances, that they have little control over their environment. People with an internal locus of control believe they can affect their environment and are more willing to try something new or different.

Then there is a *false consensus* effect. Here, people go into a situation with predetermined opinions and seek out information that supports their point of view, making it look as though they are making a rational decision based on facts. This false consensus effect is called *confirmation bias.* Another false consensus topic is *selective recall,* in which we remember only those experiences that reinforce our assumptions or decisions. In *biased evaluation,* we quickly accept any analysis that supports our opinion while subjecting evidence that does not support our opinion to very tough standards and reviews. We are all familiar with groupthink, in which there is pressure to agree with everyone else.

The second P is the problem of internal politics that stands in the way of disclosing faulty procedures or analyses. This occurs when the people at the top of the organization or who have great influence in the group have a flawed opinion or idea but others feel that it's a risk to challenge these people of influence.

The third P concerns the way people are paid. Many organizations pay top officials in ways that make the top officials ignore big risks. For example, millions of dollars in bonuses were paid out to people for putting risky investments and loans on the books of banks before the Great Recession of 2007–2009.

So how do we get past these organizational barriers?

I have a son who lived and worked in New York City for a few years. When he returned to Indiana, a local newspaper reporter interviewed him about what New York was like compared to Indiana. Of course the comparison was stark. New York is a 24-hour city where you can find and do just about anything you want at any time you want: entertainment, recreation, culture, sights and sounds, history, and on and on. Indiana, on the other hand, has hours. Things close down at some point and open at pretty standard hours. Most of Indiana is rural, so the entertainment, recreation, culture, and so forth are more limited. New York City is growing; Indiana is not, so what, the reporter asked, has to happen for Indiana to compete, to grow, to change? When I first heard my son's response,

I thought it was a little strong. Now, even though I think it could have been stated better, I think the general idea was pretty accurate. He said that the "kings of Indiana" had to die off so the younger people could take over.

In essence, we have to get the right people and the right processes in place. In organizational behavior, that means we need to start at the top with the boards of directors. They should represent diversity in ideas, backgrounds, experiences, and life views. They need to bring perspectives to the organizations that are much different than those perspectives normally considered by management. The senior advisors and other top officers and officials who surround the boards need to be given immunity and encouraged to challenge the sacred cows of the organizations, and they need to have the stature and ability to have their challenges taken seriously. Outside "counselors" or consultants can fill some of these roles, becoming the people who are hired specifically to badger, even irritate, management, forcing them to defend with facts, information, and sound philosophy the ideas that management espouses. In this environment, there are no dumb questions. Sometimes the simplest questions are the most difficult to answer and the most revealing.

Having the right people works only if the roles they play are part of the calendar, the agenda, the item that is specifically reviewed at each meeting, and if ideas and actions taken are discussed and criticized, and successes are integrated into real programs and made part of the organization. There must be regular attention paid to these ideas, not just lip service. This attention must come from the top. It has to be part of a deliberate effort to make an organization's culture one that embraces change. Although this new way of thinking can start anywhere and from anybody, the top of the organization has to lead. It has to hire and manage people who drive innovation and adaptation. The psychology, politics, and pay must reward actions, actual challenges to the status quo, that make others react and change what they are doing. Steve Jobs did that at Apple by the force of his personality and the culture that he created. Eli Lilly and Company does that by giving awards to people who had ideas that failed. Fort Wayne was changed by a man going to his neighbor and asking for help cleaning up the neighborhood. Thinking and acting in new ways has to become who we are rather than some interesting anecdotes in a book. How will we know it's happening or not? We are what our record says we are.

We cannot know that what did not work yesterday will not work today. It may work, or it may not. As of today, there is no way to tell what the next grain of sand will do to the sand pile. We have passed into a new time, becoming aware of a complexity that moves on toward whatever path our actions dictate. Resilience requires us to learn and adapt rather than to do the same things over and over again expecting different results—an insane response, by Einstein's reckoning. Historian Immanuel Wallerstein wrote, "History is on no one's side. It depends on what we do."

The risk of success while being stuck in old ideas and old ways of doing things is zero. The first step toward the cure is admitting that we have a problem.

REFERENCES

Accmoglu, D., & Robinson, J. A. (2013). *Why nations fail: The origins of power, prosperity, and poverty*. New York, NY: Crown Publishers.

Blinder, A. S. (2013). *After the music stopped: The financial crisis, the response, and the world ahead*. New York, NY: The Penguin Press.

Florida, R. (2007). *The flight of the creative class*. New York, NY: Harper Collins.

Florida, R. (2008). *Who's your city? How the creative economy is making where to live the most important decision of your life*. New York, NY: Basic Books.

Gladwell, M. (2008). *Outliers: The story of success*. New York, NY: Little, Brown and Company.

Glaeser, E. (2011). *Triumph of the city: How our greatest invention makes us richer, smarter, greener, healthier, and happier*. New York, NY: Penguin Press.

Gorbis, M. (2013). *The nature of the future: Dispatches from the socialstructed world*. New York, NY: Free Press.

Keynes, J. M. (1935, 2009). *The general theory of employment, interest, and money*. Orlando, FL: Formatted for the Kindle by Signalman Publishing.

Mayer-Schonberger, V., & Cukier, K. (2013). *Big data: A revolution that will transform how we live, work, and think*. Boston, MA: Houghton Mifflin Harcourt.

Lehrer, J. (2012). *Imagine: How creativity works*. New York, NY: Houghton Mifflin Harcourt.

Miller, M. (2009). *The tyranny of dead ideas: Revolutionary thinking for a new age of prosperity*. New York, NY: Henry Holt and Company.

Mitchell, M. (2009). *Complexity: A guided tour*. New York, NY: Oxford University Press.

Putnam, R. (2000). *Bowling alone: The collapse and revival of American community*. New York, NY: Simon & Schuster.

Ramo, J. C. (2009). *The age of the unthinkable: Why the new global order constantly surprises us and what to do about it*. New York, NY: Little Brown and Company.

Rodrick, D. (2011). *The globalization paradox: Democracy and the future of the world economy*. New York, NY: W. W. Norton & Company.

Schelling, T. C. (2006). *Micromotives and macrobehavior,* Fels Lectures on Public Policy, The Fels Center of Government, The University of Pennsylvania. New York, NY: W. W. Norton & Company.

Sharma, R. (2012). *Breakout nations: In pursuit of the next economic miracles.* New York, NY: W. W. Norton & Company.

Silver, N. (2012). *The signal and the noise: Why so many predictions fail—but some don't.* New York, NY: Penguin Press.

Strogatz, S. (2004). *Sync: How order emerges from chaos in the universe, nature, and daily life.* Hyperion Books.

Van Overtveldt, J. (2011). *The end of the euro: The uneasy future of the European Union.* Chicago, IL: B2 Books.

Zakaria, F. (2011). *The post-American world, Release 2.0.* New York, NY: W. W. Norton & Company.

ABOUT THE AUTHOR

Mark Akers is an assistant professor in the School of Business at the University of Indianapolis, where he teaches economics, fiscal policy, and international business courses. He is also an adjunct professor at Indiana University, where he has won multiple teaching awards for his courses in commercial law, law and public policy, urban structure, and public management in the School of Public and Environmental Affairs and the Kelley School of Business. In addition, he teaches economics, accounting, and international business courses as a visiting professor at the Ningbo Institute of Technology in Ningbo, China, and at Zhejiang Yuexiu University in Shaoxing, China. He holds graduate and undergraduate degrees with honors from Indiana University in management, finance, and economics. He also did professional work in marketing at the University of Colorado in Boulder and in economic development at the University of Oklahoma in Norman. A former banker, Professor Akers was also Director of Economic Development for the Indiana Department of Commerce, overseeing the state's offices in Europe and Asia, and managed the programs that attracted, expanded, and retained more than 600 companies in Indiana affecting approximately 150,000 jobs. He was also Director of Public Works for the City of Fort Wayne, Indiana, and a consultant for economic development issues to several cities and universities in the Midwest.

About the University of Indianapolis Press

The University of Indianapolis Press is a nonprofit publisher of original works, specializing in, though not limited to, topics with an international orientation. It is committed to disseminating research and information in pursuit of the goals of scholarship, teaching, and service. The Press aims to foster scholarship by publishing books and monographs by learned writers for the edification of readers. It supports teaching by providing instruction and practical experience through internships and practica in various facets of publishing, including editing, proofreading, production, design, marketing, and organizational management. In the spirit of the University's motto, "Education for Service," the Press encourages a service ethic in its people and its partnerships. The University of Indianapolis Press was institutionalized in August 2003; before its institutionalization, the University of Indianapolis Press published thirteen books, nine of which were under the auspices of the Asian Programs. The Press had specialized in Asian Studies and service-learning in higher education and, as part of its commitment to support projects with an international orientation, will continue to focus on these two fields while encouraging submission of manuscripts in other fields of study.

Books from the University of Indianapolis Press
(1992–2003)

1. Phylis Lan Lin, Winston Y. Chao, Terri L. Johnson, Joan Persell, and Alfred Tsang, eds. (1992) *Families: East and West.*
2. Wei Wou. (1993) *KMT-CCP Paradox: Guiding a Market Economy in China.*
3. John Langdon and Mary McGann. (1993) *The Natural History of Paradigms.*
4. Yu-ning Li, cd. (1994) *Images of Women in Chinese Literature.*
5. Phylis Lan Lin, Ko-Wang Mei, and Huai-chen Peng, eds. (1994) *Marriage and the Family in Chinese Societies: Selected Readings.*
6. Phylis Lan Lin and Wen-hui Tsai, eds. (1995) *Selected Readings on Marriage and the Family: A Global Perspective.*
7. Charles Guthrie, Dan Briere, and Mary Moore. (1995) *The Indianapolis Hispanic Community.*
8. Terry Kent and Marshall Bruce Gentry, eds. (1996) *The Practice and Theory of Ethics.*
9. Phylis Lan Lin and Christi Lan Lin. (1996) *Stories of Chinese Children's Hats: Symbolism and Folklore.*
10. Phylis Lan Lin and David Decker, eds. (1997) *China in Transition: Selected Essays.*
11. Phylis Lan Lin, ed. (1998) *Islam in America: Images and Challenges.*
12. Michelle Stoneburner and Billy Catchings. (1999) *The Meaning of Being Human.*
13. Frederick D. Hill. (2003) *'Downright Devotion to the Cause': A History of the University of Indianapolis and Its Legacy of Service.*

For information on the above titles or to place an order, contact:
University of Indianapolis Press
1400 East Hanna Avenue / Indianapolis, IN 46227 USA
(317) 788-3288 / (317) 788-3480 (fax)
lin@uindy.edu / http://www.uindy.edu/universitypress

University of Indianapolis Press Book List (2004–2014)

Phylis Lan Lin & Cheng Fang. *Operational Flexibility: A Study of the Conceptualizations of Aging and Retirement in China* (in Chinese and English)	0-880938-51-X $12.95
Chiara Betta. *The Other Middle Kingdom: A Brief History of Muslims in China* (in Chinese and English). Chinese translation by Phylis Lan Lin & Cheng Fang	0-880938-53-6 $19.95
brenda Lin. *Wealth Ribbon: Taiwan Bound, America Bound*	0-880938-54-4 $16.95
Philip H. Young. *In Days of Knights: A Story for Young People*	0-880938-55-2 $16.95
James C. Hsiung. *Comprehensive Security: Challenge for Pacific Asia*	0-880938-56-0 $16.95
May-lee Chai. *Glamorous Asians: Short Stories and Essays*	0-880938-57-9 $16.95
Phylis Lan Lin, Editor. *Journey with Art Afar: Au Ho-nien Museum Catalog,* University of Indianapolis	0-880938-58-7 $35.00
Winberg Chai. *Saudi Arabia: A Modern Reader*	0-880938-59-5 $29.95
Rumen Gechev. *Sustainable Development: Economic Aspects*	0-880938-60-9 $34.95
Alyia Ma Lynn. *Muslims in China* (in Chinese and English). Chinese translation by Phylis Lan Lin & Cheng Fang	0-880938-61-7 $19.95
Mac Bellner & John Pomery, Editors. *Service-Learning: Intercommunity & Interdisciplinary Explorations*	0-880938-62-5 $29.95
Philip H. Young. *Sandbox World*	0-880938-63-3 $19.95
Chau Hang. *The Happy Brush: The Joy of Chinese Painting*	0-880938-64-1 $24.95

Alex Kuo. *Panda Diaries*	0-880938-65-X $16.95
Christi Lan Lin. *Symbolism of Chinese Children's Bibs: A Mother's Affectionate Embrace* (in Chinese, Japanese, and English), International Distributor	0-880938-66-8 $39.95
Kenneth Colburn & Rona Newmark, Editors. *Service-Learning Paradigms for 21st Century: Intercommunity, Interdisciplinary & International*	0-880938-67-6 $29.95
Mel Ramaswamy. *An Immigrant Celebrates America: Reflections on America through the Fresh Eye of an Immigrant*	0-880938-68-4 $16.95
May-lee Chai, Translator. *The Autobiography of Ba Jin*	0-880938-69-3 $16.95
Kevin Corn. *Forward Be Our Watchword: Indiana Methodism and the Modern Middle Class*	0-880938-70-9 $34.95
Mary Moore & Phylis Lan Lin, Editors. *Service-Learning in Higher Education: Paradigms & Challenges*	978-1-880938-71-3 $44.95
Joseph Weber & David L. Downing. *Object-Relations & Self-Psychology: A User-Friendly Primer*	978-1-880938-72-0 $39.95
Ya-chen Chen, Editor. *Women in Taiwan: Sociocultural Perspectives*	978-1-880938-73-0 $29.95
Michael Cartwright. *Exploring Christian Mission Beyond Christendom: United Methodist Perspectives*	978-1-880938-74-4 $24.95
Mark L. Akers. *Indiana (In)decision: Hoosiers at an Economic Crossroads*	978-1-880938-75-1 $29.95
Larita Killian. *Zimbabwe Bound: A Woman's Journey through Africa*	978-1-880938-76-8 $19.95
Phylis Lan Lin, Editor. *Service-Learning in Higher Education: National and International Connections*	978-1-880938-77-5 $39.95
Winberg Chai, Editor. *Why the U.S. Needs Saudi Arabia*	978-1-880938-78-2 $19.95
Michael G. Cartwright & Merle D. Strege, Editors. *Called to Unite Knowledge & Vital Piety: Indiana's Wesleyan-Related Universities*	978-1-880938-79-9 $29.95
Yu-long Ling. *An Immigrant's Journey to the West: Confucianism and Americanism*	978-1-880938-80-5 $29.95
Peter J. Witteveld. *Horner's End*	978-1-880938-81-2 $24.95

Phylis Lan Lin & Mark R. Wiegand, Editors. *Service-Learning in Higher Education: Connecting the Global to the Local*	978-1-880938-82-9 $44.95
Mark Akers. *Real-World Economics: Complex and Messy*	978-1-880938-83-6 $24.95
Iqbal J. Unus, Editor. *Muslim American Life: Reflections and Perspectives*	978-1-880938-84-3 $24.95

For book orders, contact:

Dr. Phylis Lan Lin, University of Indianapolis Press, 1400 E. Hanna Ave., Indianapolis, IN 46227

lin@uindy.edu

http://www.uindy.edu/universitypress

(317)788-3288

INDEX

A

Acemoglu, Daron, 10–11
The Age of the Unthinkable (Ramo), 2, 4–5, 6
aggregate economics, 68
aggregate expenditures (AE), 59
Amsterdam, 92
Argentina, 29
Arthur, Brian, 67
The Atlas of the Hinterworld, 48
Aukland, 93
Austin, 90
Austria, 90

B

Bak, Per, xi, 5
Baltimore, 47
banks and monetary policy, 60
Banks, David, 88–89
Barabasi, Albert-Laszlo, 36
Baranov, F. I., 72
Benkler, Yochai, 65–66
BerkShares, 62
biased evaluation, 100
biases, in organizational behavior, 99–100
big data:
  correlations in complex systems, 62–65
  correlations in components of GDP, 50
Big Data: A Revolution That Will Transform How We Live, Work, and Think (Mayer-Schonberger & Cukier), 62
Blinder, Alan, 55
bond markets, 60–61
bonding capital, 34
Boston, 46, 47, 80, 90
Bowling Alone (Putnam), 34
Breakout Nations: In Search of the Next Economic Miracle (Sharma), 9
bridging capital, 34–35
Bureau of Labor Statistics (BLS), 24, 63
business cycles:
  GDP and, 19–20, 50–54
  Keynes theory of, 55
  See also economic cycles

C

Canada, economic complexity of, 90
Carmel, Indiana, 81
catch equation, 72–73
Centers for Disease Control (CDC), 62
chaos, 38–39
Chicago, 46, 47, 77, 90, 92
China:
  as emerging nation, 17–18
  government ability on fast decisions and implementation, 75
  government and culture, 26, 28, 96
  government spending, 16
  languages in, 25
  market economic system in, 8
  openness of society and complexity, 91–92
  resistance to change and transition, 10–11
  value of yuan, 16, 20
Churchill, Winston, 13
cities:
  about complexity, 43–49
  concentrations of genius in history, 88–89
  creation of innovative economies, 44, 46, 90, 92–93
  economic development in, 78–80
  multi-use zoning in, 81–82
  real estate prices, and poor areas in, 84–85
  site value taxation, 82–83
  urban compared to rural areas, 27, 29, 43–44, 77–78, 93, 100–101

class lines in cities and regions, 47
collaboration, 44
Columbus, 10
communication, 9–10, 44
companies:
  dominance of corporations, 70
  types of, from using big data, 64
complex communities, 78–80
complex systems:
  correlations and big data, 62–65
  in countries, rich and poor, 23
  current ways of thinking, 31–33
  definition of, 33–35
  infrastructure of, 71–72
  measuring, 37
  and networks, 35–38
Complexity: A Guided Tour (Mitchell), 34
complexity, creating more, xvi, 65, 70, 71, 87–88, 90–91
concentrations of genius in history, 44, 88–89
confirmation bias, 8, 100
Confucius, 23
consumption:
  as component of GDP, 14–15, 16, 18, 19
  synchrony with other components of GDP, 49–52
contingent behavior, 34
corporations:
  dominance of, 70
  types of companies from using big data, 64
creative capital, 76–77, 79
creative class, 47, 90, 91
critical state/criticality, 5
Crutchfield, James, 41
cryptography, 37
Cukier, Kenneth, 62, 64
culture:
  in determination of rich and poor, 23–29
  and government, 96–97
  social, human, and creative capital, 76–78
currency, new kinds, 61–62

D
Darby, Michael, 47
The Death and Life of Great American Cities (Jacobs), 83
debt and total wealth, 33
decision-making:
  on consumer purchases, 18, 53–54, 58
  and organizational behavior, 99–101
Delaware, 29
democracies:
  in determination of rich and poor, 25
  innovation and unpredictableness, 32
Deng Xiaoping, 8
dictatorships, 25
discount rate, 60
diverse communities, 78–80, 92–93
Dubai, 92
dynamic networks and complex systems, 37

E
economic cycles:
  in components of GDP, 18–19, 43
  in history, 4
  See also business cycles
economic development in cities, 78–80
economic growth, relationship to innovation, 76–77, 88–93
economics as behavioral science, 24–25
Eddington, Arthur Stanley, 31
education:
  and innovative economies, 89, 91–93
  levels in cities, 79–80
Eichenbaum, Martin, 51
Einstein, Albert, 102
Elderidge, Niles, 97
elections, 32
electric grid, 45
Eli Lilly and Company, 101
Eliot, T. S., 89
emerging nations, 9, 17–18, 21
employment and workweek and hours worked, 51
The End of the Euro (Overtveldt), 45
End This Depression Now! (Krugman), 33
Endogenous Growth Theory, 89
European Union, interconnectivity in, 45–46
evolutionary biology, 97
expectations, and predictions, 67–70
exports. *See* net exports

F
fads, spreading of, 42–43
Fairhope, Alabama, 83
false consensus effect, 100
farmland, property taxation, 82–83
fast-changing variables, 73
Fed funds rate, 60
Federal Reserve (the Fed), 60–61, 67, 74
fireflies, 41
First Amendment, 95
fish population, sustainable, 72–73
The Flight of the Creative Class (Florida), 90, 92
Florida, Richard, 46, 47, 76–77, 81, 90–92
flu prediction, 62–63
foreclosures in housing market, 33
Frankfort, 92
free software, 65–66
Friedman, Milton, 68–69
Friedman, Thomas, 75

G
GDP. *See* gross domestic product (GDP)
The General Theory of Employment, Interest and Money (Keynes), 55
Geneva, 93
genius, concentrations in history, 44, 88–89
Germany, 90
Gibson, William, 3
Glaeser, Edward, 44, 79, 81, 84
GNP (gross national product), 13
Google correlation study and flu prediction, 62–63
Gorbachev, Mikhail, 7
Gorbis, Marina, 70
Gould, Stephen Jay, 97
government:
  politics as complex system, 93–97
  public policy entrepreneurs, 75
  role in economic cycles, 18–19
  role in taxation and regulation, 83
government action:
  building systems fast and flexible, 74
  and changes to components of GDP, 59–60
  policy changes and prediction, 69–70
government spending:
  as component of GDP, 14–15, 16, 19–20
  synchrony with other components of GDP, 50–51
governmental systems in determination of rich and poor, 25
Granovetter, Mark, 42–43
Greenspan, Alan, 74
gross domestic product (GDP), 13–21
  components of, 14
  formula for, 15–16
  as linear system, 38
  market equilibrium and, 56
  synchronized behavior in complex systems, 49–54
gross national product (GNP), 13
groupthink, 43, 100

H
happiness of people, 95–96
Hartford, Connecticut, 47
A Hat Full of Sky (Pratchett), 99
Hayek, Friedrich August von, 32–33
Heisenberg, Werner, 37, 43, 69
Held, Glenn, 5–6
Hemingway, Ernest, 87
herd behavior, 43
The Hidden Fragility of Complex Systems-Consequences of Change, Changing Consequences (Crutchfield), 41
history:
  China and resistance to change, 10–11
  concentrations of genius in, 44, 88–89
  and culture in determination of rich and poor, 23, 25–26
  current peace time, 6
  technology and economy, 3–4
Hodrick, Robert, 51
Holling, C. S., 67, 73, 74–75
Homeland Security, Department of, 74
Hong Kong, 92
HOUR currency, 62
housing market:
  foreclosures in, 33
  real estate prices, 84
Hu Jintao, 26
human capital, 76–77, 79
  having the right people, 101
Hungary, 90

I
Imagine: How Creativity Works (Lehrer), 46–47, 89
immigration, 89–91
Indiana:
 compared to New York City, 100–101
 economic competition with Michigan, 23–24, 26–27
Indianapolis, 36, 80
inflation:
 and monetary policy, 61
 relationship to unemployment, 68–69
information transmission and receipt in networks, 35–36, 41–42
infrastructure, 71–72
innovation:
 cities as centers of, 44, 46
 creating innovative economies, 88–93
 relationship to economic growth, 76–77
An Inquiry into the Nature and Causes of the Wealth of Nations (Smith), 3
institutions, economic, 10–11, 28–29
interconnectivity, 45, 48–49
interest rates, 60–61
Internet, 44, 70, 85
investments:
 as component of GDP, 15, 19
 planned, 59
 synchrony with other components of GDP, 49–51
IQ magnets, 90

J
Jacobs, Jane, 81–82, 83
Japan, 90
job satisfaction, 95–96
Jobs, Steve, 101

K
Kennan, George, 32
Keynes, John Maynard, xi, 52, 55
Korean Peninsula, 29
Krugman, Paul, 33

L
language, 25
Laplace, Pierre Simon, 37–38
Las Vegas, 47, 84
laws of thermodynamics, 39
Lehrer, Jonah, 46–47, 88–89
linear thinking, 32
list of factors in country's success, 6–9
locus of control, 100
London, 92
Los Angeles, 44, 47, 92

M
macroeconomics, 34
maladaptive systems, 67, 74–75
marginal efficiency of capital, 55–56
marginal propensity to consume, 55–56
market equilibrium, 56, 57–58
mash-up, 4–6
maximum sustainable economy, 71
maximum sustainable yield (MSY), 72–73
Mayer-Schonberger, Viktor, 62, 64
Measures Short of War (Kennan), 32
mega-cities, 92
mega-regions, 90, 92–93
Mexico, 90
Miami, 92
Michigan, economic competition with Indiana, 23–24, 26–27
microeconomics, 34
Micromotives and Macrobehavior (Schelling), 34
Milan, 92
Minneapolis, 77, 80, 90
Minsky, Hyman, 33
Minsky Moment, 33
Mississippi, 29
MITBBS currency, 62
Mitchell, Melanie, 1, 34, 38
monetary policy, 60–62
money around the world, 17, 18
Moritz, Michael, 48
multi-use zoning, 81–82

N
nations:
 of economic complexity, 90–91
 and institutions, 10–11
 list of factors in country's success, 6–9
 reasons for rich or poor, 23–29
The Nature of the Future (Gorbis), 70

net exports:
as component of GDP, 14–16
synchrony with other components of GDP, 50–51
networks:
and complex systems, 35–38
Internet, 44, 70, 85
social capital in, 34–35, 76–77
New York City, 44, 46, 47, 80, 90, 92, 100
nodes in networks, 35–36
synchronized behavior and, 40
nonlinear systems, 5
and chaos, 38
North Korea, 29

O
open market operations, 60–61
open-source software, 65–66
openness of society, 90–93
order from disorder, 39
organizational behavior, 99–102
overtime worked, 51
Overtveldt, John Van, 45

P
Paris, 92
pay and organizational behavior, 99, 100
peer production, 65–67, 70
Phillips, Alban William, 68
Phillips Curve, 68
Pittsburgh, 46
planned economy, 58
planned investments, 59
politics:
organizational behavior of internal politics, 99, 100
public policy as complex system, 93–97
The Post-American World (Zakaria), 6
Pratchett, Terry, 99
predictions:
correlations and big data, 62–65
on direction of business cycle, 52–53
economic, 8–9
and expectations, 67–70
of political decisions, 94–95
and uncertainty principle, 37–38, 69
Prescott, Edward, 51
PriceStats, 63
property taxation, 82–83
psychology and organizational behavior, 99–100
public policy entrepreneurs, 75
punctuated equilibrium, 97
Putin, Vladimir, 7
Putnam, Robert, 34, 36

Q
quantum mechanics, 37–38

R
rabbits, breeding, 38–39
Rajan, Raghuram, 74
Raleigh-Durham, 47
Ramo, Joshua Cooper, xi, 2, 4–5, 6, 32, 48, 66, 72, 75, 88
real estate prices, 84
recession of 2007-2009, 16, 33, 67, 100
renting in housing market, 84
reserve requirements, 60
resilience, xvi, 52, 58, 65, 73–75, 101
resistance policies, 74
rioting example, 42–43
The Rise of the Creative Class (Florida), 76
risk in organizational behavior, 99–100, 102
Robinson, James, 10–11
Rochester, 47
Romer, Paul, 89
rural areas, 9, 27, 29, 78, 93, 100–101
Russia, 7, 91

S
San Francisco, 47, 90
sand pile, 2, 4–6, 32, 46, 48, 64, 80, 87, 101
savings, 15
Schelling, Thomas, 34, 57, 94
scientists and engineers, 89–91
Seattle, 47, 77, 90
selective recall, 100
self-organized criticality, 5
Shakespeare, 88–89
Sharma, Ruchir, 9, 17
Shaw, George Bernard, 71
shocks to economic systems, xvi, 52, 56, 59, 73
The Signal and the Noise (Silver), 52, 94
Silicon Valley, 44, 48, 90
Silver, Nate, 52, 94

Singapore, 92
Singleton, Kenneth, 51
site value taxation, 82–83
slow variables, 73
Smith, Adam, 3, 34
Smith, Stephen, 89
social capital, 76–78, 79
South Korea, 29, 90
Southfield, Michigan, 83
Soviet Union, market economy, 7
spending, 58–60
spontaneous order, 39
status quo bias, 99
Strogatz, Steven, 39, 45
strong ties in networks, 35, 76–77
supply and demand, 53–54, 56, 57–58
sustainability, 71–73
Sweden, 90
Switzerland, 90
Sydney, Australia, 83
Sync: How Order Emerges from Chaos in the Universe, Nature, and Daily Life (Strogatz), 39
synchronized behavior:
- from chaotic behavior, 39–40
- of consumption, 49

synchrony, 39–43

T

taxation, property, 82–83
technological advances, 3–4, 9–10
thought experiments, 69
toilets flushing example, 40–41
Tokyo, 46, 92
Toronto, 92
Triumph of the City (Glaeser), 44, 79

U

uncertainty principle, 37–38, 69
unemployment, relationship to inflation, 68–69
unions, 27
United States:
- economic complexity of, 90
- immigration, innovation, education, and economic growth, 89–91, 93
- time to make and implement decisions, 75

urban areas. *See* cities

V

Vancouver, 93
variables, fast-changing and slow, 73
virtual companies, 85
virtual currencies, 62

W

wages, 51–52, 99, 100
Wallerstein, Immanuel, 102
war, 4, 6, 32
Washington, DC, 29, 46, 47, 90
weak (looser) ties in networks, 36, 76–77, 80
wealth in the economy and debt, 33
West Virginia, 29
Who's Your City (Florida), 46
Why Nations Fail (Acemoglu & Robinson), 10–11
Wikipedia, 66–67
Wired Science, 88
workweek and hours worked, 51

Y

Yeltsin, Boris, 7

Z

Zakaria, Fareed, 6
Zheng He, 10
zoning, multi-use, 81–82
Zucker, Lynne, 47